The Veil
and the Mask

The Veil and the Mask
Essays on culture and ideology

J. G. Merquior

With a foreword by
Ernest Gellner

Routledge & Kegan Paul
London, Boston and Henley

First published in 1979
by Routledge & Kegan Paul Ltd
39 Store Street, London WC1E 7DD
Broadway House, Newtown Road
Henley-on-Thames, Oxon RG9 1EN and
9 Park Street, Boston, Mass. 02108, USA
Photoset in 10 on 12 Times by
Kelly and Wright, Bradford-on-Avon, Wiltshire
and printed in Great Britain by
Redwood Burn Ltd, Trowbridge and Esher
© J. G. Merquior 1979

British Library Cataloguing in Publication Data

Merquior, J G

The veil and the mask.
1. Culture
I. Title
301.2   HM101   79–40256

ISBN 0 7100 0188 6

This book is for H.,

'. . . only visible by the sunshine of her soul.'

Deign on the passing world to turn thine eyes,
And pause awhile from letters to be wise.

Samuel Johnson

Thou shall not sit
With statisticians nor commit
A social science.

W. H. Auden

Contents

Foreword

When a Jane Austen heroine compares English and French national character and refers to English *culture*, she means, of course, English *agri*culture. However, the lack of the word, in its modern sense, was not accidental. Time was, when cultures were invisible. Men did have customs and ideas, and these were not everywhere identical; but the idea of a pervasive and systematic connection, encompassing individuals and endowing them with their identities and idioms, and the diffusion of this idea itself—that seems to me a modern accomplishment. The emperor was once held to be naked, to be simply himself; but this nudity is no longer available to him. Some child, Herder or other, pointed out how fully clothed in cultural comportment he was; and ever since the word was spoken, we have all suddenly seen the cultural vestments. One of the passages in J. G. Merquior's book which I find singularly cogent is his demonstration of the continuity between Romanticism and cultural anthropology, and the particular form this filiation took.

However, a sensitivity to culture is not our only accomplishment. We have also developed our distinctive ailments, our crises of legitimacy and identity. It is part of our culture (in the anthropological sense) that no man of culture (evaluative sense) is free of the sense of the precariousness of his own identity or the fragility of political and social arrangements which surround him. To be devoid of such a sense would make one socially impossible in polite society. Happily the danger is not very great, for crises of legitimacy and identity are habit-forming. I would feel quite lost if one day I woke up with a firmly rooted confidence in the legitimacy of my pursuits, of their deep roots in the nature of things, or their congruence with the social order. Without a conscience to make cowards of us all, I'd lack extenuations as well as legitimation. I should not know which way to turn. Cultural dissonance, a sense of ambiguity, of masks and veils, in J. G. Merquior's terms, is part of one's normality.

The present book is, as the author tells us, the spin-off of a larger work centring precisely on this problem, the relationship of culture to legitimacy. Only out of the richness of a culture, its assumptions and visions, can anything be legitimated; but as cultures change and diverge and are sometimes optional, *they* in turn need legitimation. It is not for us to try to guess or predict how J. G. Merquior will attempt to break out of this circle. Those of us who have thought about this question have our own recipes, and we must wait for him to disclose his own when he thinks fit. In the meantime, however, we can benefit from astonishingly erudite, elegant, occasionally tantalizing and elusive exploration of the themes, ideas and problems which lead up to this question.

J. G. Merquior is a Brazilian who has previously written and attained academic honours both in Portuguese and in French. With this work, he demonstrates his mastery of one further linguistic sub-culture of the Western world, and his intimacy with the contents of *n* intellectual ones. Such confident tracing of interrelations of ideas from worlds and sub-worlds which do not always or often meet, and their mutual introductions by so genial, fluent and perceptive a host, augur well for the final conclusion for which this is the initiation, in more than one sense. A worthy enterprise does well to start in this manner.

Ernest Gellner
Le Tholonet, February 1979

Preface

The present essays are all of them, in one way or another, related to a larger work in progress in sociology of culture, partly undertaken as a PhD thesis at the London School of Economics and Political Science and centred on the problem of legitimacy. As I came to see it, such a problem encompasses at least three crucial issues: the baffling riddles of *political* legitimacy; the more general question of the nature, function and change of legitimacy patterns *within culture at large*; and the less comprehensive, but by no means less momentous, issue of *cognitive* validity.

In these times of rampant irrationalism and mounting onslaught (from right and left) not only on scientism, the myth of science, but on science itself, the fate of cognitive legitimacy within contemporary culture threatens to become a main concern for everyone who believes in, and cares about, the objectivity of critical knowledge. In Pietro Rossi's pithy remark, we are facing a new trial of Galileo, as the number increases of those who seem, wittingly or unwittingly, to prefer Adam's apple to Newton's. For my part, I can only hope to contribute to the realization that the further we get from culturalisms and their 'humanist' premises, the nearest we come to a truly illuminating sociology of culture—a sociological branch whose theoretical framework is the main topic of the following essays.

Many a subject-matter discussed or broached in them have been personal obsessions to me since I was introduced to the human sciences, in an undogmatic, thought-provoking way, by Professor Antonio Gomes Penna, in the now so remote Rio de Janeiro of the late 1950s and early 1960s. As crucial themes in the sociology of culture they began to gnaw at me during my five-years term as a curious *profiteur* from interdisciplinary permissiveness at Claude Lévi-Strauss's seminar of social anthropology at the Collège de France, Paris. They reached the state of perfectly vampiresque incubuses during my present sojourn in Britain, where I have had the privilege of conversing with open-minded philosophical sociologists such as Donald G. MacRae and Ernest Gellner, at the LSE. I am much indebted to Professor Gellner for his critical reading of early drafts of some of these essays (especially of chapters 2 and 3). Thanks to an invitation from Celso Lafer, Francisco Weffort and Maria Victoria Benevides, chapter 1 was read as a working paper at a CEDEC seminar, in S. Paulo. I found the ensuing debate, which was further enlivened by the presence, among others, of Fernando Henrique Cardoso and Marilena Chaui, quite fruitful and rewarding. I have also greatly benefited from the generous encouragement given by Roberto de Oliveira Campos, who took a lively interest in most of the genuine, and in some of the false, problems I struggled with. This book, the first I dared to write in English, encapsulates in a sense a kind of literary catharsis for which, nevertheless, none of them can be held in any way responsible.

J.G.M.
London, 1978

1 The veil and the mask: on ideology, power and legitimacy

1 The symbolic of complex society

Ideology and legitimacy seem closely related. Exploring the nature of their connection is arguably one of the most rewarding approaches to the sociological study of both. Ideology is widely thought to permeate the operation of principles of legitimacy within society, as well as the collective awareness thereof. In the eyes of the sociologist the phenomenon of legitimacy is to a great extent nothing but ideological thought in conspicuously binding form. Bindingness, as stressed by Max Weber in his classical discussion of Part One of *Economy and Society*, is a distinctive mark of legitimate orders.

Now, in so far as the analysis of legitimacy claims to be sociological, and hence empirical-minded, it can hardly be expected to engage in any speculative enquiry into the 'intrinsic' aspects of claims to validity. Rather, it is bound to focus on the signs of practical recognition of a given normative order. In other words, recognition, whether stemming or not from 'belief', must be ascertained in behavioural terms. Moreover, legitimacy creeds cannot help appearing from this viewpoint as sets of ideas deeply enmeshed in the social process—and as such, quite distinct from 'pure' mental constructs to be scrutinized regardless of their social embodiment.

Because it concentrates on the social rooting of ideas instead of focusing on their intrinsic meaning, the sociology of ideology provides an invaluable path to explaining the functions and change of legitimacy patterns. Conversely, given the considerable breadth of the overlapping of legitimacy and ideology, the study of the former, if properly conducted, helps us to understand some crucial dimensions in the role of ideology itself, which is the main topic of the present chapter.

However, some theorists seem to believe that what happens between ideology and legitimacy is less a functional overlapping than an outright identification, in which ideology is practically subsumed under legitimacy. Let us follow their reasoning for a while.

Patterns of legitimacy, it is argued, are first and foremost sets of collectively held beliefs about validity. The psychological ground of legitimacy is in fact the recognition of the validity of a given social norm. Legitimacy patterns are therefore analysable into value-statements enjoying group acceptance. Social behaviour is indeed governed by what anthropologists and sociologists alike call *value-orientations*. These we may describe, following Kluckhohn, as explicit or implicit generalized structured conceptions, shaping behaviour, of man's place in the world and man's relation to man.[1] Underwriting this concept of value-orientation, Smelser described values as 'the most general statements of *legitimate* ends which guide social action', norms being the embodiment of such statements.[2]

On the other hand, legitimacy beliefs, in their intrinsic involvement with value-orientations, are more often than not couched in the language of 'social symbolism'. Social symbolism, in turn, might be deemed the lingua franca of value-orientations— and it was the very density of the symbolic at the heart of culture that made social symbolism a major concern of the sociological mind, from Durkheim and Sapir to Lévi-Strauss and Victor Turner.[3]

Now, *ideology* is, first and foremost, a kind of social symbolic endemic to, if not wholly exclusive of, 'complex' societies, especially in their modern subtype, 'class society'. The relationship between ideology, legitimacy and the symbolic has enjoyed for some time now full citizenship in sociological theory. Parsons (*The Social System*, ch. 8) identified ideology with the 'cognitive legitimation of patterns of value orientation', and Deutsch related legitimacy to the compatibilization, operated through the use of symbols, of discrete actions, aiming at the achievement of x values, with the key values within the social system. Legitimacy is the effect produced by the association of experience with value-laden symbols—symbols, that is, carrying authority in virtue of their representing core values in their culture.

Some recent re-definitions of ideology are equally outspoken in pointing out its intertwining with legitimacy. Thus Seliger writes:[4]

> An ideology is a belief system by virtue of being designed to serve on a relatively permanent basis a group of people to justify in reliance on moral norms and a modicum of factual evidence and self-consciously rational coherence the *legitimacy* of the implements and technical prescriptions which are to ensure concerted action for the preservation, reform, destruction or reconstruction of a given order.

No careful reader will miss an important difference between the Parsons-Deutsch line of thought and Seliger's definition. For the latter, the peculiarity of ideology as a belief system lies in its *connection with group interests in a given social order*. This *sectional* nature of ideology *qua* belief system may be deemed the central tenet of ideology theory proper. The absence of the sectional perspective is the reason why some otherwise very fruitful models of explanation of thought by society are of little avail as regards the analysis of ideology.

To mention the most seminal of these models: all that Durkheim, in the *Elementary Forms of Religious Life*, asserts about the causal relation between society and thought focuses clearly on a holistic relationship, not on a sectional one. This holistic bias does not even suffer from the ambiguity of formulation in Durkheim's thesis of a social causation of the 'categories of the understanding'. As Lukes has pointed out, the ambiguity can be considerably dispelled if we realize that everything hinges on how we are to define society.[5] If, as Durkheim often does, we conceive of it as a 'collective consciousness', consisting of mental representations shared by all the socii, then the determination of thought by society is a kind of spiritual Parthenogenesis, hardly able to inspire empirical research: if thought as society is taken to engender thought as the conceptual order, there is little for the empirical social scientist to undertake here. If, however, society refers to a morphological and/or institutional structure, then the thesis of a determination of thought by society becomes the basis of really interesting, testable hypotheses. Even though Durkheim was largely mistaken in

3

thinking that logical categories and logical principles mirror some aspects of social structure, the *logical* structure *of his theory* makes a lot of sense, and has proved ever since quite fertile as a research programme.

Let us mention very briefly one or two conspicuous examples of the explanatory suggestiveness of the Durkheimian perspective. One is Gluckman's explanation of witchcraft beliefs by the particular kind of social interaction underpinned by tribal social structure, which, as we shall see (cf. pp. 73–4), qualifies as a sound infrastructuralist approach to the sociology of culture. We could hardly think of a better instantiation of a holistic, non-sectional sociology of belief, devoid of any appeal to the mystery of 'collective consciousness'. Another, far more controversial, example of holistic 'sociology of knowledge' would be Lévy-Bruhl's famous speculations about the societal background of logico-scientifical thinking. According to the author of *La Mentalité primitive*, a differentiated social order, whose prototype was the social structure of classical Athens, based on conscious agreement between its individuals rather than on tradition, is a pre-condition of every breakthrough of logical (as opposed to pre-logical) thinking. Although, as it has been noticed,[6] such a conception is sharply dissimilar to Durkheim's own way of correlating thought and society (since, for Durkheim, the analysis of the structure of primitive society explains *both* the so-called pre-logical *and* the logico-scientific modes of thought), it is nevertheless equally holistic. Less concerned about the 'nature of society', more straightforwardly an evolutionist than Durkheim, Lévy-Bruhl modulates the thought-society equation along history; but he, too, conceives of the social term of the equation as a social whole, never as a section of the social fabric.

Refraction of thought, then, through the interests of a given section of social structure seems to be the core of ideology theory. The sociology of ideological formations deals with the multifarious entanglements of thought with clusters of interests; and the *interest nexus* is what provides ideologies with their differentia specifica among the various kinds of collective beliefs. We shall presently consider the main conceptual and empirical problems most often involved in such an 'interest theory of ideology', but before proceeding any further, we must dispose of at least three gross general misconceptions, frequently to be found in the vast, less sophisticated literature on the subject. These are the totalistic fallacy, the epiphenomenalist illusion, and the crystallization bias. Let us briefly consider each one of them.

(a) The totalistic fallacy consists in the preposterous opinion that *all* social thinking is socially determined, in a way basically analogous to the manner ideologies are.

The 'total' conception of ideology was a typical product of idealism in the guise of the strongly culturalist 'sociology of knowledge' of Karl Mannheim (on which see pp. 64–5); accordingly, it presupposed the tacit obfuscation of the links which tie ideology as sectional thought to a *structured* dynamics of social stratification (admittedly not only economic) and the identification of ideological beliefs with 'world views' actually imputable only to the high culture of an intellectual élite taken to be the spiritual representative of a given social class. Modern reappraisals have done away with this patently arbitrary notion. Class ideologies could scarcely be 'total', if only in virtue of their *rhetorical* function: they need to employ a basis of common codes of communication in order to address themselves, in the (often unconscious) hope of persuasion, to other classes;[7] nor are they to be detected and scrutinized solely at the level of their high-brow crystallizations in élite culture.[8] (Even some dimensions of thought which are eminently social *cannot* be reckoned contingent upon social evolution in this sense. Take, for instance, the 'code' aspect of natural language (what Saussure termed 'langue', in opposition to the individual speech-act, or 'parole'): no matter how high the likelihood of a strong social conditioning of its immemorial origins, the code of natural language works for ages and ages as an essential prerequisite of social life, much more than as a product of it.)

(b) The epiphenomenalist illusion is, of course, the tendency to treat ideology as sheer epiphenomenon of social reality. The fact that ideologies are socially determined by no means implies that they are superfluous 'reflections' of their social bases.

Ideologies, any more than ideas, are implements of society, not redundant ghosts. They could hardly ensure the fostering and protection of group interests if they were no more than passive duplications of other social data. As Giddens, commenting on *The German Ideology*, puts it, ideology is illusory in so far as beliefs invested with universal validity are in reality the expressions of

5

sectional class interests, 'not in the sense that the content of idea-systems is a mere "reflection" of material life and therefore is irrelevant to the activity of the subject'.[9]

Besides, it is not enough to acknowledge the functionality of ideology, as does Seliger in his definition, as regards a *given* social order. We must go further than that and be ready to admit the occurrence of what one would feel tempted to call (if the term sounded less pedantic) *coenogonic* thought (from 'koinos', common + 'gonia', begetting): in other words, thought that, *without prejudice to its being socially conditioned*, nevertheless helps *creating* social processes, well beyond the mere legitimation of action aimed at the 'preservation, reform, destruction' of any given order (a less rebarbative hybrid would be 'socioplastic').

A good example of 'coenogonic' ideology is the role of nationalism in prodding German bourgeois élites into industrialism in the mid- and late nineteenth century. As D. S. Landes, one of the most authoritative experts in the economic history of that period, has stressed, the German bourgeoisie soon learned to gain social status by patriotically contributing to national aggrandizement through a vigorous handling of manufactures directly or indirectly linked to state power (such as coal and iron, engineering, and later chemicals and electricity), in a country wilfully geared to national self-assertion since the near annihilation of its leading region, Prussia, at the hands of Napoleonic France. Unlike most of its French contemporary counterpart, the German bourgeoisie displayed an industrializing ethos which in the event proved decisive for the radical transformation of the country's economy in an astoundingly short time.[10] While we can easily reckon this entrepreneurial nationalism a status-seeking strategy, thus relating it as an ideology to a situational 'basis', no attempt at seeing it as a 'reflection', or even as an interest-preserving device, would do: for German nationalist industrialism preceded, instead of followed, the formation of a large-scale industry (until the mid-century, Germany had remained a typical backward economy), and the interest nexus was, in this case, of a rather prospective nature. So the functionality of ideology can quite often surpass helping preserve a 'given' order. Without ever being demiurgically omnipotent, ideologies can turn out to be undeniably creative.

(c) Finally, the crystallization bias consists in the habit of restricting ideology to its articulate or crystallized forms.

Neither literate conspicuousness nor doctrinal coalescence is a sine qua condition of ideological occurrence. Ideologies are as often as not conveyed by several kinds of unwritten gospels—'secular scriptures' (sometimes even unavowed 'codes' of manners) underlying the cognitive, practical or expressional conduct of a given group. Consequently, in the analysis of ideology, one should always take care not to miss the spirit because of too much concern with the (frequently absent) letter.[11] As Pierre Bourdieu's sharp warning has it, 'the most successful ideological efforts are those which have no need of words, and ask no more than complicitous silence' (*Outline of a Theory of Practice*, p. 188). Concentrating (as does, for instance, Seliger) on *political* ideology—on the 'forensic' as distinct from 'latent' ideology, to adopt R. E. Lane's useful terminology[12]—often effects this kind of restriction, to the detriment of a more comprehensive sociological explanation of ideological creeds.

2 A modest vindication of interest theory

Let us now look more closely at our defining element—the interest nexus. Modern papers on ideology are increasingly prone to distinguish two main approaches to its study: interest theory and strain theory.[13] Both these concepts are at the same time psychological and sociological, referring as they do to psychic relata such as the realization of advantages, or to states of psychological tension, as well as to social ones such as objective chances or socio-cultural dislocations; but they differ decisively concerning the function of ideology. For interest theory, says Geertz, 'ideology is a mask and a weapon'; for strain theory it is 'a symptom and a remedy'. The first links ideology with the pursuit of power; the second, with the flight from anxiety.

Unfortunately, interest theory is too often bent on espousing either a crude utilitarian psychology, in which man is implausibly driven by impeccable rational calculations of his own real or possible advantages, or then a fuzzy historicist expressivism, in which ideas are unconvincingly (because vaguely) said to be expressions of social positions and historical circumstances.

As for the best-known interest theories which are *not* committed to the shortcomings of rationalist psychology, they could hardly replace their utilitarian rival, because they do away with the *social* determination of thought. To take the most influential of them,

7

that of Nietzsche: Does it not patently play down, if not ignore, the sociological concretum where the universal will-to-power—the main Nietzschean independent variable—operates? Nietzsche's 'genealogy of morals' constitutes an exploration as stark as subtle into the manifold guises of a crucial facet of ideology—its deceiving, *masking* effect. Moreover, in his writings, the uncovering of the masking function of ideology goes hand in hand with another central aspect in ideological processes: the *unconscious* nature of the use of thought-masks. In none of them, however, do we find a sustained attempt at a theorizing of the intrinsic *social* linkage of unconscious intellectual masking. Nietzsche saw in the will-to-power a universal drive constantly disguised beneath a variety of vital masks, but self-differentiated along largely overlapping occupational, ethnic or religious types (the warrior, the priest, the artist, the Greek, the Jew, the German, the English, the Christian) only *contingently* connected with a societal basis: that is why, for all the shrewd psychologist, and even social psychologist, he was, he remained closer to his beloved great moralists in the French classic tradition than to a truly sociological critique of ideology. (This limitation does not, of course, prevent us from fully acknowledging the relevance of Nietzschean perspectives concerning the interpretation of several trends in modern European culture.)

The case of Pareto is somewhat more equivocal. In his huge *Treatise* he concentrated on the social role of non-logical ideas. These contain a constant element, or 'residue', and a variable one, the 'derivation'. Residues are half a dozen basic predispositions lying at the root of human activities of non-logical nature, and as such are distinct from material wants or 'interests'. Derivations are the masks of residues, which are the true factor in human conduct. Moreover, while residues differ from society to society, their distribution among the social strata of each society also changes significantly, especially in regard to the paramount differences between élites and the ruled.

So it would seem we have all the ingredients for a sociological theory of 'derivations', whose similarity to ideology is more than conspicuous. In the event, however, Pareto gave us nothing of the sort. He stressed the psychological differences between élites and dominated groups, as well as between élites themselves, at the expense of their relations to the class structure. As a rule his élites are never positionally reckoned; that is, never defined by an analysis of their place within a series of interwoven social and occupational positions underpinned by structures of wealth, prestige and power. The very sameness of residues throughout history accentuates this lacuna. Though residues are not instincts, being partly socially conditioned, they remain substantially the same throughout history; one class or another of residues may become hegemonic in society, but the residues themselves do not change, nor are they inherently plastic vis-à-vis the diversity of social formations.[14] If sociology is to be the study of derivations, it cannot help being self-defeating: for the key to derivations is a theory of residues, and residues owe next to nothing, in their nature, to social reality. It may be unfair to accuse Pareto of seeing society as changeless but there is plenty of reason for considering his 'sociology' guilty of psychologism. His aim was unquestionably sociological; his achievement, quite unsociological—a criticism that holds also, in my view, against the decisive role of an 'impulse-structure' (Triebstruktur) in Scheler's 'Soziologie des Wissens'.[15]

At any rate, the chief weakness of the interest theory of ideology lies perhaps less in its crude psychological portrayal of its beneficiaries than in its inability to account for the *acceptance* of ideological beliefs by non-benefiting groups. If ideology is just a 'rationalization' of class interests, then how is it also believed by those who do not share in the advantages it rationalizes? Here, apparently, strain theories fare much better. In maintaining that all societies are chronically mal-integrated[16] since they all know incongruences between the goals and norms of their sub-systems as well as contradictions between the role expectations generated therein, and in viewing society, consequently, as a gigantic drama fraught with tensions that require at least an easing through imaginary solutions,[17] strain theorists seem to offer a sensible answer to the riddle of ideological assent: for, according to their view, *all* groups within society benefit from the (temporary) acting out of social tensions: ideology is a carnival of the collective mind, and as in every carnival, everybody takes part in it.

Do they indeed? The notion that belief-constructions can be a safety-valve for the ever-mounting tensions of society, or a balm providentially poured into the wounds opened every now and again by the sundry frictions between its heterogeneous elements, is undoubtedly plausible. The only trouble is that in it, ideology becomes a predicate of society *as a whole*. By the same token, it

9

loses that connection with sectional interests in which we see the hallmark of ideological beliefs. Significantly, Geertz (op. cit.) locates the main theoretical grounding of the strain theory of ideology in Parsons's 'Freudian' elaboration of Durkheim's systemic conceptions.[18] Ideology is seen as the catharsis of social dislocations, the abreaction of the entire social system.

In other words, strain theory is holistic by birth and character. In fact, strain theory deserves the name of *epistemological holism*, for it is holism only in so far as it reflects the point of view of the social whole, without that assumption of a mythical patternedness held by the so-to-speak 'ontological' holism of functional or configurationist anthropology (for the criticism of this assumption, see pp. 45–53), for, according to Geertz (or to Lévi-Strauss), there is no contradiction in positing belief-systems as functions of *society* and refusing to see the latter as something endemically well integrated.

However, the plausibility of strain theory at the systemic level does not appear to extend to every kind of society. Strain theory may reasonably explain some tension-managing processes in primitive or archaic society (hence its appeal to anthropologists like Geertz, the Java expert, or to Carlton, who draws heavily on Geertz's theorization and applies strain theory to Ancient Egypt's thought) but it can scarcely yield the same explanatory results when dealing with class society, with its multiple and often conflicting belief-systems. At bottom, the superiority of strain theory over the interest nexus explanation as regards the problem of ideological assent is largely an illusion since, as the viewpoint of the whole comes to prevail, the difficulty of accounting for the acceptance of ideological beliefs on the part of non-beneficiaries simply does not arise. Actually, strain theory does not solve the problem of ideological assent—it just bypasses it.

The moral of all this is plain enough. If strain theory is immaterial, as far as the sectionality of ideology is concerned (or, in other words, it is relevant only as long as the omnibus concept of ideology, which is useless for our analytical purposes, is retained), then the interest nexus is less easy to dismiss than it seemed at the beginning. In his 1960 survey of ideology theory since the war, Birnbaum, noticing that a 'renunciation of discussion of the question of interests' was a conspicuous trend in the literature, attributed the decline of interest theories to the impact of end-of-ideology social thinking as much as to the intrinsic difficulty of the subject, and concluded by welcoming a revival.[19] Today it would seem that some minimal theoretical conditions for such a revival have been put forward.

The most important among these conditions is a re-definition of the interest nexus that would solve the above mentioned enigma of ideology: How can a belief held in the interest of some be shared by others? In the tradition of ideology theory this intriguing phenomenon is termed 'false consciousness'. Classical Marxism, the father of the sociology of ideologies, contained at least two ways of looking at false consciousness.

The first, vividly expressed in the *Communist Manifesto*, focused on the cheating of the subordinated class by the ruling one; thus the bourgeoisie masters the 'ideological apparatuses' (to borrow Althusser's terms), thereby preserving such a hegemony (Gramsci) within the civil society that it seldom needs to employ the coercive power of the state to preserve its rule. As the resounding slogan has it: 'The ruling ideas of each age have ever been the ideas of its ruling class.'

The second Marxist portrayal of ideology is more subtle. In it 'false consciousness' applies to the ruling class itself, ideology being a *socially determined* occultation of the actual motives of class behaviour. In Marx's penetrating historical study, *The Eighteenth Brumaire of Louis Bonaparte*, the predicament of the petty-bourgeois peasantry is largely accounted for in terms of *this* sort of false consciousness. Here the ideological veil is no longer, properly speaking, a mask; self-delusion of the social ego prevails over any deceiving of an alter. Class interest remains the main prop of false consciousness but the latter, instead of being artfully inculcated in the minds of exploited groups, is first and foremost unwittingly experienced by the very dominant ones, who cannot help perceiving their social world this way. Ideology ceases to be a lie to become an unconcious belief.

Marx himself, in a celebrated paragraph of *The Eighteenth Brumaire*, warns against the 'narrow-minded idea' that the French petty-bourgeoisie acted on a conscious basis of selfish class interest. On the contrary, the petty-bourgeoisie of 1850 believed that its emancipation represented the only way of avoiding class struggle and saving modern society from the threat of painful disintegration. Thus the false consciousness of the petty-bourgeois peasants or shopkeepers, and of their political representatives (who, by the way, are far from being all originated from the petty-bourgeoisie) is not a function of any transparently self-

11

conscious class interest—rather, it is a function of the limits imposed by their 'life-activities' upon their ways of conceiving social reality.

It might be argued that ideology as false consciousness—as a set of perceptual barriers imposed by the social structure—has also a much wider meaning in Marx's thought, the locus classicus of the meaning being the famous 'fetishism of commodities' depicted at the end of the first chapter of *Capital*. The greater width of ideology as commodity fetishism, as compared with the false consciousness of the petty-bourgeoisie in *The Eighteenth Brumaire*, shows itself most conspicuously in that it comprehends *all* classes involved in 'reification', i.e. in an unwitting assent to a state of affairs in which everything—including, ultimately, human relations—takes on the reifying character of a commodity.

Lukács made the fetishism of commodities into the very starting-point of the 'Reification and the consciousness of the proletariat', the central essay in his *History and Class Consciousness* (1923). Yet in the impressive amount of critical scrutiny of this book, rightly reckoned to be the cradle of 'western Marxism', little attention has been paid to the fact that *Marx*'s fetishism of commodities is *not* presented as a form of false consciousness specific to capitalism, let alone to the capitalist class (hence the modest role it plays in *Capital*, in the logic of capitalism as a historical process). Lukács somewhat glossed over this aspect by pronouncing reification to be the 'prototype of all forms of objectivity and their corresponding forms of subjectivity' in 'bourgeois society'.

Now while such a conflation says much about the young Lukács's debt to Simmel's Verdinglichung (a crucial notion in the latter's *Philosophy of Money*) as well as, more generally, to Weber's rationalization drive, it scarcely chimes with the class-boundness of ideology in the central Marxian sense. 'Fetishist' reification as a forma mentis of money economies is for Marx just one of the generic pre-conditions of a fully fledged class society, that of capitalism, and as such it remains closer to the more historical specimens of holistic social thought (like Lévy-Bruhl logico-scientific thinking) than to the sectional creeds which alone properly constitute ideologies. Not surprisingly, it has been used and abused to underpin many a woolly disquisition on the pervasiveness of alienation but it has not inspired any noticeable study of the relationship between thought patterns and social strata. For this very reason, we must leave it aside from the present discussion.

Thus classical Marxism possesses, as it were, a *two-sided image of false consciousness*. On the one hand it states false consciousness is the blindness of the exploited as regards the reality of their plight; on the other it asserts it is the inability of even the exploiters to overcome the limits imposed upon their vision of the social being by their class location. (False consciousness is equally, of course, a major aspect of another central Marxist concept, that of alienation, but we shall refrain from going into it in the present discussion.)

What needs to be stressed is just that the second Marxist notion of ideology as false consciousness gives a new depth to that interest nexus which lies at the root of ideological beliefs. This is the view commented upon by P. Hamilton when he writes that 'ideology . . . is not produced to "cover up" reality in a conspiratorial fashion, but is systematically generated by the structure of social relationships'.[20] Jean-Marie Vincent speaks of a 'spontaneous myopia'[21] a partial cecity dictated by the position of a class within a set of social relations (which, of course, underlies the surface networks of social interaction). Compared to such *structural* determinations of class belief, *apologetic* forms of ideology and, in particular, the 'explanatory obsession' of ideological propaganda (despite the insistence of some authors[22] on considering it a major feature of ideology) are quite uninteresting. Behind the theoretical reduction of ideology to apologetics and propaganda, there lurks a *conspiratorial* notion of group interest, but conspiratorial interest robs the social scientist of the rewarding excitement of uncovering the hidden springs of collective behaviour. The uncovering is exciting because *these* motives are covert—but it is rewarding because they are far more decisive in terms of social causation than the intentions of social actors. As we all know conspiracy theory is but a poor explanans of social dynamics.[23]

The sociological grounding of false consciousness can be served as a strong or a weak thesis. Its strong version claims that the boundaries of socially determined class thinking are absolute. This is quite untenable, given a host of glaring counter-factuals—of which Marx and Engels themselves, the arch-antibourgeois with impeccable bourgeois pedigrees, are only the most notorious example. In its weaker version, however, the notion that most of the social views of people are to a large extent moulded by their class position has proven sound enough. At any rate, it is prima facie far more acceptable, on empirical grounds, than the uncanny assumption of any thorough inculcation of alien beliefs in subordinated classes—the 'opium-for-the-masses' idea of ideology, whose long but rather unilluminating career, since the *Communist Manifesto*, we have already mentioned.

The structural view of false consciousness purges interest explanation of ideology from the shallow utilitarian psychology and conspiracy theory of society, which aroused so many justified criticisms.[24] By the same token, it undermines the argument of those who, throwing the baby out with its bath-water, cling on to the shortcomings of an opium-for-the-masses variant of interest theory as a pretext for doing away with the interest element altogether. When, for instance, Stark invites us to interpret the famous Marxian tenet that it is men's social existence that determines their consciousness as a *denial* that 'interests', as a mere by-product of social existence, have any determining force,[25] he is simply twisting Marx's ideas in order to get support for his wilful rejection of ideology theory in the name of the 'purer' problems to be dealt with by a sociology of knowledge unstained by any debunking-bent image of man. In Marx's own thought, for all its sketchiness in this particular area, the determining role of social existence by no means obliterates the fact that interests are at stake. The unconsciousness of interest does not annihilate the power and privilege structures of class society. We do not have to forget that interests steep in the objective realities of class inequality (economic or not) to shun the fallacy of rationalistic psychology and the myth of conspiracy.

Nevertheless, our main question is still unanswered. By incorporating a sense of social structure into its account of ideology, interest theory became respectable; *yet it left unexplained the interest/acceptance nexus*. Granted that class interest is seldom a conscious matter, and society scarcely the object of wily manipulations—even so, what makes people apparently conform to beliefs demonstrably foreign to their own interests? What on earth account for *voluntary* compliance with social norms on the part of the unprivileged? At least, the false consciousness of superordinate strata is a sectional set of beliefs reflecting, however obliquely, their *own* vested interest in a given social order (though not in everything which is 'given' in it); but what happens when the (basically) *same* false consciousness seems to be shared by those who have no share in its interest basis?

14

If, following Althusser,[26] we reply that every social formation needs to reproduce its own *relations* of production (as much as its *forces* of production), such a reproduction being ensured by a set of 'ideological apparatuses' (church, school, family, political parties, press, arts and letters, etc.), we still fall wide of the mark; for all this explanation provides is a *Why?* which says next to nothing about the mysterious *How?* Indeed, how do the ideological apparatuses manage to brainwash the masses? After all, church and family, party and press are far from being always *unilaterally* committed to ideological inculcation. Very often, they strongly support *opposition* to the ideology of the establishment. Even if they actually did, all the time, completely and consistently indoctrinate the masses with beliefs fostering social conformity, then how is it that dissent and rebellion are as conspicuously present throughout the very social setting where churches, parties and media normally operate? Taking the cloud for the goddess, Althusserianism—in many ways, a Parsonianized Marxism—collapses here into a fallacy analogous to (though not identical with) that of normative determinism (see p. 64): it imprudently infers, from the (largely supposed) ideological *purposes* of some institutions, the unwarranted conclusion that they actually *succeed* in converting people to ideological belief.

Perhaps the only way out from the seemingly insurmountable difficulties of explaining ideological acceptance outside class interest is to turn the tables and boldly to forget about the 'enigma of belief'. Since every 'mentalist' approach to the problem of ideology-sharing appears to be bound to fail, *a behaviouristic perspective* seems worth trying. Is there a way of studying the working of ideology *otherwise than primarily as a belief*? Fortunately yes: it consists in seeing ideology as part of the empirical mechanics of *power*. Was not the 'pursuit of power', after all, another name for 'interest' as the main prop of ideology?

In point of fact, the modern analysis of power is of itself conducive to ideological theory. The analytical study of power, in recent times, roughly corresponds to the critical progress leading from Dahl's *Who Governs?* (1961) to Bachrach and Baratz's work, epitomized in *Power and Poverty* (1970) and hence to Steven Lukes's 1974 *Power.*[27] Put in a nutshell, it amounts to the following steps.

(a) First, reacting against Wright Mills's sweeping assertions

15

about 'power élites', Robert Dahl equated the study of power with the analysis of *observable* decision-making processes (and then concluded that, in the case of the USA, there exists a pluralist polity and not any unified power élite); this is what Lukes calls the 'one-dimensional' view of power—a view fundamentally *liberal* in its philosophical outlook.

(b) Second, Bachrach and Baratz, criticizing Dahl, directed attention to the crucial importance in power processes of '*non*-decisions', that is, of (covert) decisions to the effect of excluding vital issues from the agenda of politics. This is the 'two-dimensional' view of power, *reformist* in outlook.

(c) Finally, Lukes, criticizing in turn the Bachrach and Baratz approach, offered a three-dimensional conception of power. The basic assumption here is that people can be socialized into accepting a false view of their own interests but that this subtle power mechanism operates through a 'mobilization of bias' within a given political system that normally outreaches the realm of intentional choices (which non-decisions, being a special kind of decisions, also are, in so far as they are made by those who profit by it). Actually, this mobilization of bias, profitable for vested interests, steeps in mechanisms that are 'neither consciously chosen nor the intended results of particular individual's choices'.[28] This would be a 'third-dimensional' view of power, *radical* in outlook.

Not surprisingly, this last, three-dimensional view of power asserts the relevance of exertion of power through concrete forms of thought control (notably control of the media, or of agencies of socialization). Furthermore, while stressing *latent* (as distinct from actual) conflict, it underlines the objectivity of interests—especially in the occurrence of contradiction between the interests of those exercising power and the interests of those *excluded* from a given benefit.[29] Last but not least, the notion of latent conflict actually *presupposes the first concept of false consciousness* discussed above, since what keeps conflict of this kind latent is the (temporary) inarticulateness of the real interests of those excluded from decision-making.[30]

At first sight, the three-dimensional picture of power raises a serious theoretical difficulty. The common-sense view of power makes it inseparable from intention and decision-making. Power, as classically defined by Russell, is 'the production of intended effects'. Bearing this in mind the liberal Weberian, Dennis Wrong, stresses the need for distinguishing two sub-categories of influence: social control and power. Social control, something to a degree inherent in every social interaction, denotes the diffuse, unintended influence exercised by society over socialized individuals. Power, on the other hand, 'is identical with *intended* and effective influence'.[31] By the same token, whenever we are in the face of *internalized* social controls, Wrong believes the concept of power 'clearly inapplicable'—[32] a proposition unlikely to be underwritten by any believer in power (also) *as ideology*.

Lukes's main retort to the inevitable objection arising from the Weber-Russell (and John Smith) idea of power consists in a general onslaught on the 'behaviouristic' theory of power, which, identifying the latter with decision-making, leaves in the shadow an enormous amount of power phenomena in society.[33] Since we started this discussion of ideology as power in order to evade the entanglements of the belief theory of ideology, and in so doing promised to contrast the behavioural focus of power theory with the mentalistic approach of belief theory, I had better hasten to add that Lukes uses 'behavioural' in a derogatory way *only* in the sense of studies of power focusing on 'concrete decisions' in so far as they are instances of 'overt and actual' behaviour; otherwise, as he himself explains, he has no quarrel with a behaviouristic approach.[34]

Ultimately, then, Lukes's analysis of power is far from 'mentalist'. Just as our discussion of ideology was forced to elide the question of *belief*, the 'third-dimension' view of power puts into parentheses the issue of *will*. Lukes's best argument in favour of regarding ideology as power bears witness to it. He claims that the imputation of responsibility for the effects of the exercise of power does not always require the occurrence of deliberate conduct; for there are plenty of instances, like cases of negligence, 'where we hold people responsible for actions they did not decide upon'.[35] At bottom, this argument may be regarded as an extension of the modern juridical idea of responsibility. In the words of Collingwood we might say that, for Lukes, one good proof of the existence of a non-decisional level of exercise of power is that the law holds people responsible also for some 'events', not only for their 'acts' proper. Intention is immaterial; damage, suffered within a social relation (such as a *labour* accident), highly relevant.

The three-dimensional view of power must also face some

empirical difficulties. Lukes himself has recognized that the empirical identification of real interests checked by the third dimension of power, i.e. by *power as ideology*, raises several problems. He submits that, ultimately, such an identification must be left to the putative victims' expression of their grievances through the active freedom afforded by participatory democracy.[36] Thus the truth of power underneath its ideological veil lies in a likely, though not inevitable, praxis of social protest. Conversely, the determination of the truth of interest depends on the same future praxis, not in any positivist analysis of the given.

The notion of a third dimension of power looks perfectly compatible with our concept of ideology as a sectional, interest-driven belief-system, more often than not unconsciously held. As for Lukes's qualms about the empirical detection of victimized interests, one cannot but applaud their moral cautiousness. How very much do they differ from the arrogance with which radicals lecture people about the grievances they ought to feel! Notwith-standing, in a way these scruples restrict too much the field of operation of power as ideology available for sociological scrutiny.

A broader, largely similar, conception of ideology as power strategy has just been put forward by the anthropologist Abner Cohen. Cohen's starting-point is a shrewd realization of the present state of anthropology. Evans-Pritchard once wrote (in his *Social Anthropology*) that the concern of the anthropologist is with 'problems, not peoples'; and Geertz reminded anthropologists, not so long ago, that they 'don't study villages—they study *in* villages'. In line with these warnings, Cohen thinks that nowadays, when 'ethnography is no longer news'[37] and anthropologists begin to accept intellectually, if not ethically, the ineluctable disappearance of segmental, and shrinking of traditional, societies, it becomes imperative to realize that the commitment of anthropology to the so-called microsociological level regards only *its techniques*, not its theoretical scope.[38]

Now, as Cohen sees it, the main subject-matter of anthropology in its capacity as the microsociology of *complex* society should be *symbolic strategies set up by interest groups*, the symbolic of power emanating from informal (and often 'invisible') interest groups, like ethnic cousinhoods (e.g., the Hausa in Ibadan, or the Creoles in Sierra Leone), occupational élites (the City of London Victorian Jewry), or secret ritual brotherhoods (Freemasonry). Taking issue with the Weberian propensity to reduce power to state politics,

Cohen is keen on detecting patterns of symbolic action performed by these groups, relating them to a structure of objective interests within power relations.

The similarity of such an enterprise to the analysis of ideology is self-evident. The only important difference is that Cohen's microsociology focuses on middle-range groups instead of relating power symbolism to classes (or to primary units, based on face-to-face interaction). However, this makes his approach complementary, rather than contrary, to class ideology theory: it is simply a question of graduating the range of our analysis of sectionality, depending on whether belief and symbolism express the situation of a larger or of a smaller stratum. The hub of it all—sectional refraction of thought through a largely unconscious interest nexus moulded by the structure of social stratification— remains essentially the same in both perspectives, whereas the identification of interests acquires an empirical basis far more tangible than Lukes's hypothetical detection of damaged interests through democratic participation.

Lukes and Cohen help us to conceptualize ideologies as power strategies. In so doing, they also help us to retain—without stumbling on the enigmatic problem of ideological acceptance by non-interested groups—the truthfulness of interest theory and, in particular, of the accent it places upon the sectional character of ideological belief. While the focal interests in Lukes's three- dimensional view of power are those of the *victims* of ideology qua power, Cohen prefers to highlight the other end of power relations, focusing on the interests of power-holders (although some of his ethnic examples occupy rather the middle ground). In both writers, however, power (whether political or economic) generates interests, or, then, interests are power-seeking, generating in turn symbolic strategies to preserve or foster themselves. The hallmark of such symbolics is precisely their being vehicles for the sectional refraction of belief through interest. That is what makes them, most typically, ideologies.

Having so conceptualized ideology as power, we must now try to grasp its underlying mechanics. Indeed the importance we have attached to the difference of perspective between Lukes and Cohen has been dictated by the need for empirically ascertaining power configurations as the explanans of ideology. As it happens, however, Cohen's theorization, *if taken at an explanatory level*, turns out to be quite unsatisfactory. Since the social situations

19

which give rise to power-driven symbolics are never analysed within the framework of a detailed portrayal of a given power structure, it is even hard to avoid the impression that power dramas, as the vis a tergo of such symbolics, are simply inferred from the latter—in which case ideology analysis would fall wide of a true sociological explanation.[39] Therefore, in order to be more specific about the power/ideology connection, we must look for *a more structured view of power situations*, after which we shall conclude by returning to the relationship between ideology and legitimacy.

3 Power, ideology and legitimacy, or, exit belief

The recent theoretical reshuffling of the sociology of power by Roderick Martin provides us with the broad lines of such a structural view of power in society.[40]

Martin begins by drawing a critical assessment of the two most influential concepts of power in the literature, that of Weber and that of Parsons. The Weberian concept of power can be summarized as the capacity of A to get B to do something that B would not otherwise accomplish. Martin agrees with Parsons that such a concept contains an inbuilt assumption of conflict: the definition implies that the interests of B are being sacrificed to those of A, thereby ignoring the possibility of mutual convenience.

Surprisingly, he also takes Weber to task for his alleged tendency to transpose power as a property of interactions into a property of actors.[41] What worries Martin is that defining power as an individual property eases the way for misleading notions of power in terms of 'generalized capacity' rather than in terms of a specific relationship—precisely the view taken up by Parsons, for whom power means, as is well known,[42] a generalized symbolic medium which, operating in society in a way analogous to money, and being as such endowed with an essentially cumulative, non-zero-sum nature, secures the performance of binding obligations legitimized by their reference to collective goals. Martin rightly accepts the criticism of Giddens[43] that this amounts to treating power as legitimate by definitional fiat, and to starting from the assumption of consensus between power-holders and their subordinates. In brief, Parsons, who blamed Weber for ignoring the possibility of interested consent, unabashedly converts consent into a consensus as aprioristic as Weber's conflict, which at least had the merit of being much closer to the intuitive experience of power.

20

For Martin, *power relations* rest upon two elements: 'asymmetric patterns of dependence' resulting from differential control over access to desired resources and the greater or smaller availability of 'escape routes' to subordinates.[44] Control over desired resources is in turn, needless to say, contingent upon the distribution of natural goods, the level of technology, and inheritance customs, the desiredness of resources being, for that matter, an obvious cultural variable.

Besides, four phenomena are constantly associated with power[45]: (a) *compliance*, non-self-regarding behaviour performed at the behest of others; (b) *coercion*, the application, or threat of application, of physical deprivation in case of non-compliance; (c) *authority*, which is legitimized domination, norm-bound and marked by the consent of the subordinated to perform non-self-regarding actions; and (d) *influence*, which is a form of domination employing neither coercion nor authority (for example, bureaucrats may comply with the wishes of their superiors without granting any legitimacy to their orders and, of course, without being threatened by any physical deprivation but only, let us say, out of fear of loss of future promotions).

It is worth comparing this typology of power forms with that of Bachrach and Baratz.[46] The latter had also defined *coercion*[47] by the threat of deprivation, *authority* by legitimacy based on consent, and *influence* by the power of A to change the course of action of B without resorting to the threats of 'severe deprivation' but also without B recognizing the legitimacy of the command.

Bachrach and Baratz, however, propose a further concept, that of *force*. In a power situation involving force, the objectives of A are *not* achieved, as they are in a coercive situation, by the compliance of B under threat of deprivation; rather, they are achieved in the face of the non-compliance of B. In coercion it is still B who, in spite of everything, chooses what to do; in force, by contrast, it is always the power-holder alone. Force strips the victim of power of choice between compliance and non-compliance. Finally, force is also irrational and non-relational. Under the duress of force there is only a *minimal* interaction between A and B, since the former's objectives are to be achieved without any proper 'transaction' between them. To illustrate: if, in a 'Your money or your life' predicament, B surrenders to A, we have coercion; but if A has to kill B to get the money, power becomes force.

Although Bachrach and Baratz do not mention David Easton in their book, their contrast between force and coercion coincides strikingly with Easton's sharp distinction between the *threat* of force and the *exercise* of force. The latter in turn had a forerunner in Simmel, who insisted that whereas even the strongest, tyrannical coercion is always relative, for it always implies some degree of choice on the victim's side, physical violation is precisely the only species of the power kind where domination destroys the subordinate's freedom to comply or not.[48] However, the main point, to our purpose, is that Bachrach and Baratz consider *manipulation* as a form of force, not of coercion, since the subject in the grip of manipulators has no choice as to course of action[49]: he does not choose between compliance or non-compliance; if he 'complies', he does it in full ignorance either of the source or of the nature of the demand forced upon him by a power-holder. Like coercion, force and manipulation involve a conflict of values; but unlike coercion, they tend to be non-rational and non-relational.

Power situations differ according to the degree of dependence, the ease of escape, and the relationship between these factors.[50] Martin discerns four basic configurations in this connection:

(a) too asymmetric a dependence coupled with easy escape encourages the use of *coercion* to secure compliance;
(b) too asymmetric a dependence with little chance of escape, on the contrary, stimulates compliance based upon *authority,* because subordinates will normally try to avoid physical deprivation by consenting to their subordination, whereas power-holders will find authority cheaper and more effective than coercion;
(c) a less pronounced dependence with easy escape also leads to compliance resting on *authority*, since to a great extent compliance can only be obtained with the subordinate's agreement;
(d) lastly, if dependence is not too imbalanced, but escape proves difficult, compliance is likely to be grounded on *influence.*

What of ideology and legitimacy in all that? Power configurations defined by coercion or by 'influence' (in the sense given to it by Bachrach and Baratz, and Martin) do not make any room for legitimacy feelings on the part of subordinates. On the other hand, authority is notoriously the primary link connecting power with legitimacy. Yet, as we have just seen, there is a big difference between power configurations characterized by (c)—low dependence and easy escape—in which case the exercise of power needs to get the subordinates' consent, and power configurations like (b) where high dependence is combined with little possibility of escape, for here consent is much more a means by which subordinates, resigned to their dependence, try to preserve their own dignity by avoiding coercion than it is the product of a genuine belief in the legitimacy of power. (Incidentally, this seems to me far more important to sociological analysis than the *psychological* ambiguities of the 'Erlebnis' of authority (where submission is voluntary, yet is experienced as compulsory) by which theorists like Blau and Wrong[51] set such great store). In brief: *if there cannot be authority without consent, there can exist consent without legitimacy*.

Now, in the case of ideology as the 'third dimension of power', we have downright manipulation, that is to say force, however subtly exercised. Clearly there is no room here for legitimacy beliefs either. Manipulated consciousness can be manipulated through that in which it has faith—but the *power* exercised through manipulation is never in itself an object of belief as such. Manipulations are always '*hidden* persuasions'.

Of course, the word 'manipulation' has too bad a semantics for an analysis trying to rehabilitate interest theory by reshuffling the category of false consciousness. It seems much more adequate to the vocabulary of those conspiratorial accounts of social dynamics shared (with only a change of villains) by vulgar Marxists and right-wing witch-hunters alike. What is, nevertheless, of paramount relevance is to abide by the essentials of the technical meaning just mentioned, and to regard manipulation as a 'spiritual' version of force, that is, of power, exercised in a situation where there is no conscious choice on the part of the power-subjects.

Power in its 'third dimension', i.e. power as ideology, obviously qualifies as such 'spiritual' force. Moreover, its consubstantiality with power tout court becomes particularly visible if we apply to it an older, but no less useful, classification of power dimensions. As we recall, de Jouvenel also discerns three dimensions according to which we can graduate power:[52] its *extensiveness* (according to the number of subjects), its *comprehensiveness* (according to the range of actions to which power-agents can move subjects) and its *intensity* (according to the range of options available to the power-holder within each power relation). There is no doubt that ideology is in principle a vastly extensive and amply comprehensive kind of power, although the exact extent to which this is so will always be an empirical matter. As to the question of intensity, the very kinship between ideology and (non-physical) force constitutes a self-evident answer.

Contemporary social theory already shows some inclination towards reverting to the Parsonian habit of transmuting the base lead of power into the gold of legitimacy. Stinchcombe, for one, re-defines legitimacy as the extent to which a power can be effectively backed up when its holder calls upon other centres of power; legitimacy is a *power reserve* which generates stability because it rests on the credibility of probable action in support of specific acts of power.[53]

In the same vein, Stinchcombe imputes the social effectiveness of values (and legitimacy is, as we have recalled at the outset, a value-symbolic) to a high correlation between commitment *and power*.[54] Institutions are for him, above all, loci of concentrated power committed to some value or interest. He argues that the Parsonian concept of institutions, based on the idea of role expectations, cannot provide an explanation of the historical continuity of such corporate entities; the persistence of institutions is much better clarified by Selznick's insights into the politics of survival deployed by administrative leadership.[55]

Moreover, given this causal efficacy of institutions with regard to the enforcement of values, a historical macrosociological generalization suggests itself: while the social strength of values in simple societies, lacking great concentrations of power, will usually rest on value commitment, in modern societies, rich in institutions, institutional power, rather than disembodied commitment, becomes of paramount importance. The survival of typical value-clusters like religion bears witness to this: for instance, Protestantism survived where Protestant kingship (a typical power-cluster) won, vanished where it lost.

If I may be permitted to sum up the background of this theoretical issue with the help of two harmless neologisms, I would say that Parsonianism led to its culmination an *archic* mood, whereas an author like Stinchcombe exemplifies a *cratic* reaction. 'Archic' theories love to think of power phenomena in terms of a hallowed authority, the venerable arche which means at the same time 'origin' and 'principle'. Authority is for them less a power *over* than a power *from*—the august emanation of a sacred source located, if not literally, in tradition (archic thinkers are not necessarily archaic-mongers), at least, philosophically, in the very nature of things. Unfortunately, imbued with such an aural spirit, the archic mind tends to refrain from facing the cruder realities of cratos—of coercive or constraining power. Only too prone to seeing legitimacy everywhere, the archic priests are constantly oblivious of the existence of *il*legitimacy—let alone of its sad companionship with inequality and oppression. Understandably, the archic mentality knows next to nothing about ideology as interest-driven power symbolic. Ideology is for archism only authority writ large, widespread legitimacy; its primary concern is not with divisive interests but with integrative values. Ideology is, functionally considered, a lay religion, and religion is—the archic thinkers are fervent neo-Durkheimians—the cement of society.

In real life, of course, things are more often than not slightly less noble. Even the rare really holistic ideologies, such as nationalism, are permeated by strong class ingredients. No doubt class thought seldom remains secluded in the walls of class. Surface, conspiratorial, opium-for-the-masses ideologies (be they concocted by wealth or by party oligarchies and state bureaucracies) are born infiltrators: they address themselves, by definition, to the gentiledom. It is not only ideology *as mask* that transcends the limits of class, however. Unconscious interest-belief, false consciousness structured by the social process rather than by conspiratorial will—in other words, *deep* ideology, to wit, ideology *as veil*—also frequently crosses class borders. The bearing of such trespassing on legitimacy is worth meditating on.

Consider again, just for a while, Abner Cohen's symbolic strategies. These were developed from within the cousinhoods of the Creoles of Sierra Leone and of the Victorian Anglo-Jewry as a way of legitimating power and status. Such a legitimation could either take the form of a preservation of their social authority, like it happened with the Creoles, or—in a rather 'coenogonic' drive—it could work chiefly so to speak before the event, like the cousinhood of the City Jewry, which helped promote new levels of status for the Rothschilds and Samuels, Montagus and Henriques, who had suffered until the early nineteenth century from several civic disabilities. Moreover, the legitimizing effect of these ideologies had a *dual* function. On the one hand it legitimated these groups in their own eyes; on the other, it legitimated them, to a degree, in the eyes of the larger society.

The notion of *class ideal*, advanced by the historian Harold Perkin, aptly describes this double pattern—this *double-edged legitimacy*. For Perkin, the class ideals of the three main classes in the first period of industrialism performed two things. First, *sublimating* the crude interests of competition for income, they sanctified the role of class members by justifying the claim of their class to a special place in society, thereby acting as catalysts of class formation. Second, by trying to undermine their confidence in their own ideals, they operated as an instrument of propaganda or psychological war as regards the other classes.[56]

One side-effect of this sublimation of the competition for income into a struggle between distinct class ideals is, incidentally, as Perkin recognizes, to make it possible for people to embrace ideals alien to their economic situation—the shifting that was so vividly illustrated, in the Britain of the last century, by a David Ricardo, the landed enemy of land property, or a Robert Owen, the capitalist who turned into a spokesman of the working class.

Still, even when the ability of sublimating class ideals to lure people away from their 'normal' class beliefs is fully granted, the decisive point about ideological belief remains the fact that the core of belief is always on the part of those whose objective interests coincide (however indirectly and unconsciously), by and large, with that which ideology praises. The intensity of ideological belief seems to be highly centripetal: the closer one comes to its class basis, the more intense it is.

Most of the seeming counter-examples to this—such as the notoriously greater disaffection towards conservatism in the upper classes, as contrasted with the 'traditional' middle ones—are quite misleading, for they invariably misread the actual interests of the 'betraying' classes. The upper classes in advanced capitalism 'know' what they are doing when they espouse liberal ideas, since the liberalization of capitalism as a class society is closely linked with its capacity for survival. The 'betrayal of the élites' is a Paretian nightmare with only dwindling chances of application to modern society. Elites, in the most plastic and resilient social formation ever set up on earth, have to be highly adaptive—or perish.

Class ideals, then, may sublimate class interests—they do not cancel them. In so far as they also address themselves to other classes, they exude a double-faced legitimacy aura—one for the self-validation of their class of origin, the other for attracting the moral support of alien, frequently antagonistic, groups. There seems to be no historical example of equivalence between these two faces of ideology as regards the intensity of belief: wide and strong credence remains invariably attached to its natural class-core—natural, that is, in as much as it constitutes a cluster of interests that set a class apart within society as a whole.

It is therefore not at all surprising that ideology, working generally as a *veil* to its normal class-bearer and conveyer, often appears as a *mask* to most people outside it. The aura of belief is brighter around the strata whose interests each ideology represents (without merely reflecting them); the farther one gets from the seat of interest, the dimmer the halo of credence tends to become. Hence the difference in the moral optics of ideology: for, while both ideology as veil and ideology as mask are distortions of social reality, they are seldom perceived as *similar* distortions. What the veil and the mask hide, they do not conceal the same way. Once ideology freed, the member of a superordinate class sees the ideals of his own class as a self-delusion; but the external observer, especially when he grasps the power content underneath these same ideals—when he sees them as power-biased—cannot help taking the unconscious veil for a purposive mask, deliberately worn by a dominant class as if it were only too overconscious of class warfare. As long as power encroaches upon balanced exchange in social intercourse, ideological veils will go on being uncovered as though they were ideological masks—and this, quite apart any variation at that surface level where masking ideas are actually made up, in conspiratorial fashion, as (ig)noble lies.

In its normal sociological depth, however, ideologies should be seen as veils, rather than masks, *that connote power without denoting it*, and conceal the manipulation of subordinate consciousness *without necessarily strongly appealing to belief on the part of the latter*. This would quite agree, for that matter, with recent studies on lower class mentality. It has been suggested, for instance, that modern workers in advanced capitalism, not very long ago hastily thought to be embourgeoisified, actually display a curiously pragmatic attitude towards dominant values, in the sense of values of the dominant classes: they seem to accept the prevailing value system whenever they find themselves faced with general, abstract issues—but they tend to resort to a clearly 'negotiated' version of such a value system, or then to stick to their own class values, whenever they experience 'concrete situations involving choice and action'.[57]

Besides, even the acceptance of such negotiated versions of prevailing values should not be hastily regarded as a proof of deep belief in them; for it may well be the case that the acceptance of dominant values by subordinate classes results to a large extent from the relative inarticulateness of *alternative* value-sets, rather than from any genuine internalization of other classes' moral standards. The study of *linguistic deprivation* provides us with a striking (if, admittedly, extreme) illustration of such a faute-de-mieux credence. As Martin remarks, the work of sociologists of language such as Basil Berstein and, following him, Claus Mueller, argues very persuasively for the possibility that categories of speech within the poor vastly restrict the intellectual scope of their use of language.[58] Such categories allow for a grasp of the hic et nunc of class experience but they scarcely support less immediatistic assessments of the poor's situation and long-term interests. The pragmatic contemporary workers discussed in the preceding paragraph are definitely not on a par with these paupers; yet the impact of linguistic deprivation on class consciousness is still a world-wide phenomenon, especially acute in most of the developing countries.

Any would-be sociological theorization of legitimacy patterns which would ignore it would certainly run the risk of portraying ideology (no matter how strongly it would keep deriving the latter from a class origin) in ways regrettably similar to the romantic myth of 'organic' complex societies. Just as, in the romanticized mediaeval Christendom, classes were said to 'commune' together in the same creeds—without, of course, anyone taking pains to check, on the base of even a minimal empirical procedure, which 'beliefs' were really held by the massively inarticulate peasantry—so those who equate ideology with belief tend to *assume*, rather unwarrantedly, that acceptance means faith on the part of subordinate strata (very often, belief theory limits itself to translate organicist assumption into the hackneyed language of class; Althusser's concept of ideology, for instance, is a curiously Durkheimianized Marxism—and, as we shall see in the next chapter, Durkheim owed very much to romantic holism).

Significantly, modern social history finds it wiser to operate at a far remove from the crude assumptions of belief theory concerning lower strata. Wallerstein, for one, is remarkably cautious about the extent of legitimacy creeds. As he tackles the problem of political legitimacy in Renaissance Europe, he notices how doubtful it is that very many governments have been considered 'legitimate' by the majority of the ruled (and, more often than not, exploited). After all, he thinks, governments are seldom supported: most of the time they are just endured.[59] As for legitimacy, it concerns less the masses than the cadres, since it depends primarily on the greater or lesser ability of the small number of people managing the state machinery to convince larger administrative and regional groups of the soundness of their policies.[60]

All in all, one general conclusion seems forcefully to emerge: *as far as belief is concerned, ideological legitimacy is chiefly, though not exclusively, for internal consumption*. Its function is really to act as a catalyst for the mind of the group whose interests it sublimates into a justificatory set of ideals. In so doing, the catalytic sublimation veils, rather than consciously masks, the realities of sectional interest. Outside the interest-bound class circle, ideology consists primarily in a set of unchallenged, normally tacit, value-orientations which, once translated into the language of purpose, amounts to that 'manipulation of bias' in favour of privileged groups.

Needless to add, the class ideal is not always just a passive sediment of credos and assumptions; in many of its forms, it works more as a dynamic *energeia* than as a static ergon. Even when deprived of what we termed a coenogonic bent, ideology frequently acts in history as an *idea ideans*, rather than as a simple idea ideata. Returning for a moment to Lukes's third dimension of power and to A. Cohen's symbolic strategies, it is not difficult to see that the former corresponds to ideology as ergon, the latter to ideology as energeia.

In the history of Marxist thought, the writings of the young Lukács and those of Gramsci[61] strongly stressed an *active* image of ideology. The *Utopian* Marxism of the last mid-century—from Ernst Bloch to Cornelis Castoriadis—is obviously an hyperbolic variety of such a dynamic notion of ideology. Bloch's avowed millenarism, Castoriadis's 'imaginary institution of society' turn creative into demiurgic ideology; but these are extreme cases of Marxism's periodical return to its idealistic philosophical sources.

Marxism is still, as a rule, blamed for being a dogmatic infrastructuralism which allows little room for the specific creativity of ideological superstructures. On closer inspection, however, a certain Marxism proves as keen as, say, Weberianism on stressing the coenogonic or socioplastic role of ideology. A book such as *History and Class Consciousness*, the fountainhead of Western Marxism, and the kernel of Gramsci's more theoretical prison fragments, bear witness to this. No wonder the young Lukács was remarkably influenced by Weber (who had been his teacher at Heidelberg) and Gramsci deeply obsessed by the dedialecticized Hegelian spiritualism of Croce. When all is said, then, we are led to the conclusion that what renders Marxism highly problematic as an instrument of ideology analysis (no matter its capacity as the main inspiration of *class* theory) is not its long overcome unwillingness to acknowledge the creativity of ideology but rather its persistent inability to rescue class analysis from the grip of a long-discredited philosophy of history. Even Gramsci's flexible concept of *hegemony*—so close in spirit to the ideology-as-power perspective—rests on a largely mythical, rather than truly historical, ideal of bourgeoisie and proletariat. The Althusserians, while dropping the more encumbrant relics of a messianic class struggle prophetism, did not on the other hand evince the slightest inclination towards real empirical-minded analysis of social structure, as it is easy to see in the arbitrary formalism of the class taxonomy of Poulantzas's *Classes in Contemporary Capitalism*.

Let us not be too rigid, however, about the reduction of legitimating belief to the class kernel of ideology. Recognizing that, outside the logic of interest, ideology is less a matter of active credence than a question of unexamined class-biased assumptions experienced unawares by subordinate groups whose own interest runs counter to them does *not* preclude the acknowledgment of some very significant *social uses of belief*. Durkheimians regard belief as not only a means of social control but as one truly *constitutive* of society; in the last analysis, they conceive of society as coextensive with its value-laden 'conscience collective'. Other theorists, nevertheless, refusing to consider belief (at least, in the strong sense) as essential to social life, prefer to take creeds as just an agency of control. Gellner's emphasis on the social function of unintelligibility, or even of downright absurdity,[62] is a case in point. Belief controls conduct through unintelligibility, through blocking the egalitarian effect of understanding. That is why customs steeped in inequality often soak in absurdity: many a rule of etiquette, many a deferential rite—one has only to think of

Veblen's rich catalogue of leisure-class symbols—would probably not work so well if they could be made rational.[63] Now these crypto-political credos are clearly ideological: they spring from unconscious power symbolics of dominant groups, not from any Durkheimian sacralization of the cohesive virtues of belief. In fact, Gellner's sociology of the absurd (the so-called 'bobility' thesis in his essay, 'Concepts and society') goes together with a resolute rejection of the idea that fideistic belief is a necessary condition of *any* successful social arrangement. Actually, it does not even refrain from surmizing that we, the inhabitants of an incipient 'pragmatic rather than absolutist, technical rather than adaptive, mathematical rather than verbal' civilization may very well be entering an age characterized by the eclipse of belief. In such a world 'a credo will become as archaic as a totem'.[64]

It is worth comparing these bold views on the mortality of 'belief culture' (with its cool realization of the recess of the verbal element in cognition[65]), with Topitsch's remarks on the erosion of anthropomorphic thought forms in industrial civilization, where science did away with the anthropomorphic projection of ethico-political meanings on to cosmos and society, which was a hallmark of religious and philosophical thinking. In particular, sociomorphic analogies, supported by the overwhelming role of natural language as a theoretical idiom, ceased to provide models for generally accepted interpretations of reality.[66]

At all events, the rise and fall of the 'culture of the word' (Gellner) and its bearing on the fate of the humanistic intelligentsia is a theme bound to become a favourite topic of a historical sociology of culture. What requires underlining is just the criticalist[67] demotion, and debunking, of the role of creed in society. While for a Durkheimian the mere expression 'belief culture' is a tautology, all culture, in the sense of society, being by definition made of beliefs, Gellner's neo-Enlightenment sees the social credo quia absurdum as an instrument of that unconscious (but highly functional) 'manipulation of bias' which we found at the root of ideologies as power symbolics.

4 Concluding remarks

The identification of ideology as a power symbolic seems to be the best way to grasp the nature of ideological thinking as sectional, interest-driven thought forms. However, identification has at most heuristic, not explanatory, value. In order to *explain* ideology sociologically, one must, as unequivocally as possible, do two things:

> (a) relate convincingly the ideological forms to power configurations and hence to classes or similar groups (that amounts to the supply of those 'connectives' which Merton justly blamed Mannheim for neglecting); and
> (b) relate in turn the classes or similar groups to the larger structural processes operating at the level of the entire social system itself.

Admittedly, at bottom, this move amounts to almost converting ideology analysis into an overall sociological explanation. To a certain extent, indeed, there is no gainsaying that such a structural anchorage of the study of ideology makes it into a kind of synecdoche of the analysis of social system; but the question is: can it be avoided, if the deep dynamics of class structure are to be really understood? Which other analytical item would enable the study of ideology to remain faithful to our infrastructuralist methodological precept—as one has indeed to do, if one is to observe the logic of reduction demanded by scientific explanation? (See chapter 3.)

The real logical and methodological imperative in this connection will always consist not in trying to maintain the study of class thought artificially isolated from the grasping of larger social processes but rather in preventing the sense of the functional specificity of class ideology from getting lost or diluted in the necessary reference to the broader picture of social dynamics as a whole. No easy task, to be true, but not an impossible one.

Basically, the relationship between ideology and analysis resembles that between figure and background. The secret of a successful explanation of ideology resides in its being able to take into account the background social processes without which the ideological figures do not take on their full 'visual' meaning and, at the same time, in its capacity never to lose sight of the figures themselves. The motto of it all could well be: nothing is in (class) ideology which was not previously in the underlying social process, except the ideology itself.

The more accurate literature explicitly or implicitly dealing with the problem of sociologically explaining ideology indicates that the real breakthroughs in class analysis are closely connected with one kind or another of systemic approach. This is also partially true of some recent ambitious contributions to ideology theory whose main thrust is historical, with a strong focus on the peculiarities of ideology in advanced capitalism, such as Adorno's, Habermas's, Bell's or, just now, Gouldner's.[68]

In so far as ideologies are class symbolics, they are to be explained by their social support; but this in turn demands to be explained by the development of larger structures, the global social formations. The golden rule of class analysis seems therefore to be the spelling out of the *primacy of process over class*—and that is a rule that only a diachronic-minded structural sociology can fully obey. Its no less important corollary implies a special sensitivity to the incongruences between class purpose and class function within the social system; for, as Karl Polanyi forcefully stresses in his classic study of the social context of market economy, *The Great Transformation*, 'the fate of classes is much more often determined by the needs of society than the fate of society is determined by the needs of classes'.[69]

It goes without saying, notwithstanding, that neither this golden rule nor its corollary should ever be taken as a licence to lapse into that panfunctionalist fallacy denounced by Merton, and present every ideological manifestation as the embodiment of some function useful to the social system. In ideology analysis the sense of system should be moderated by the realization that, very often, the power arrangements underlying ideologies as power symbolics work rather as 'compensatory mechanisms', i.e. as devices to compel continuance of services for which there is little functional reciprocity—a point well argued by Gouldner.[70] It is, indeed, indispensable—and such would be our second general explanatory commandment—that the sense of 'fittingness' in the systemic approach necessary to locate the causes of class formation does not cancel the sense of asymmetry essential to grasp the reality of power.

Whenever ideologies present themselves as sublimating class ideals (but this is by no means the only aspect they take), they propose a curious problem to sociology. Indeed, sociology is more often than not the study of *unintended* but *efficient* social action. In ideology as class ideal, on the contrary, we very often find examples of *intended* but *inefficient* action.[71] This is just one among the many fascinating challenges ideology offers to the sociological mind.

The essentially critical concept of ideology has been the great historical underminer of several myths of legitimacy: much of what had been said and done in the name of legitimacy turned out to be, on closer inspection, no more than the prejudice of privilege, no matter how creative this was in history. It does not seem far-fetched to suggest that a good deal of the alleged 'crisis of legitimacy' in our time may be to a considerable degree an ideological bogus. However, this is an issue to be tackled and tentatively answered through a discussion of historical legitimacy patterns. For the moment, it is preferable to conclude by summing up our central contentions about ideology and its bearing on legitimacy.

We may begin by recalling that not all thought is socially determined, nor all socially determined thought ideological (rejection of the totalistic illusion). On the other hand, ideology has definitely a social function (it is no epiphenomenon); not seldom, it works as an active force in society; occasionally, it may even acquire a qualified capacity to generate societal structures ('coenogony'). Moreover, its social function extends beyond its more articulate 'crystallized' forms.

Now, ideological thinking, as has been argued, is always *sectional*; it is to be predicated of groups (mainly classes), not of society as a whole. The first duty of ideology theory nowadays is therefore to recover the sense of group false consciousness determined by social structure and social process. By the same token, it must regain the ability to discern ideology as an unconscious veil distorting the image of social reality within class and sublimating its interest-basis, not as a conspiratorial mask consciously employed to deceive social subordinates. The full restoration of the concept of false consciousness—the reinstatement of 'veil' ideology—is crucial. To a certain degree, it represents a return to some basic insights of classical Marxism, to which, as Merton says, we owe the decisive shift from the psychological to the social plane in the study of ideology. By the same token, it also amounts to rejecting Lenin's equation of ideology with the conscious creed of an élite (the revolutionary party) instead of with the unconscious assumptions of dominant, or power-seeking, larger strata (although the sublimatory side of ideology in Lenin's sense is surely not worthless for the study of 'class' ideals of revolutionary parties transformed into omnipotent state bureaucracies). It is significant that Lenin, in outlining his own, more Paretian than truly Marxist, notion of ideology,[72] was deeply indebted to Kautsky's vindication of 'the *conscious* element', while the *unconscious* has always been a key aspect of the sociological concept of ideological belief. Lenin also got rid of the interest dimension, which was to be still more resolutely rejected by Sorel's activist notion of ideology as a totally irrational 'myth'.[73]

The Pareto-Lenin-Sorel view, with its basic disregard for class determination, also lurked behind the famous (and highly ideological) 'end of ideology' dicta (the so-called Shils-Lipset-Bell thesis of the late 1950s and early 1960s)[74] for which the ideological amounted to political sectarianism, not to a thought form (sectarian or not) essentially related to group interests.

Moreover, the sociological approach alone can guarantee a critical distance from face-value (or face-meaning). Unless we 'reduce' ideology to class position in a specific social structure, we shall never understand, for example, why the 'same' individualist creed so closely attached to the rise of capitalism in the West was, in Ming China, an ideology of Mandarin bureaucracy, directed *against* incipient 'bourgeois' capitalism. A methodologically infrastructuralist sociology teaches us to recognize that such ideologies were only *apparently* identical; as functional class symbolics, they were in fact quite different.[75]

Finally, the motivational link between social position and ideology is provided by the role of sectional interest in asymmetric social arrangements, asymmetry being viewed as the result of power configurations. It has been suggested that group interests are ultimately to be detected by an analysis of power, not by a scrutiny of belief. Internalization of dominant class values by subordinate classes turned out to be largely a false problem. Acceptance of ideologically legitimized rule proved capable of dispensing to a great extent with internalization, just as consent proved to be vastly independent of legitimacy belief. Whenever we adopt a 'cratic', realistic view of power (instead of indulging in 'archic' sublimations of coercion, influence and manipulation into legitimate authority), we cease to regard ideology as the vehicle of unanimous legitimacy beliefs and see it as the instrument of an appropriation of a rhetoric of legitimacy by power-holding or power-seeking groups. The fact that such an appropriation operates through unwitting mechanisms and unrealized assumptions makes it only more effective—and all the more attractive to the sociological eye.

Lest this should be misconstrued, it is better to add at once that we have no intention whatsoever of denying the importance of value-internalization in social life. In every social situation one needs to interpret, gauge and evaluate information to ascertain the meaning of what is happening in order to build one's response— and all the more so in situations of co-operation or conflict. This already involves a minimum of value-projection, since one's interpretation of what is happening will broadly reflect one's previously internalized standards. To the extent that these are moulded by one's social position, and to the extent that these internalized sets of values work as *self-validating*, being normally immune to that *decentring* drive—from self-images to objective truth—inherent, as we shall see (p. 69), in scientific cognition, value internalization is ideological.

Even so, as attitude theorists willingly recognize, beliefs do *not* have clear effects on actual behaviour.[76] Besides, the very existence of internalization renders the whole issue even more complex, for, as the psychologist, L. B. Brown, reminds us, 'the response to ideologies is . . . personal although their basis is social'.[77] How could it be otherwise, given the fact that adaptation is (in Newcomb's phrase) a 'three-pronged problem', comprehending a necessity for coming to terms with not only the others and the social world one shares with them, but *also* with one's own 'intrapersonal, autistic demands'? We should be careful not to take internalization as a one-way process.

During the last fifteen years, the more blatant trends in ideology theory have stemmed from 'semiotic' anthropology and 'structural' Marxism. The central problem of the former is, according to Geertz, to explain how ideology 'transforms sentiments into significance'[78]—for which an awareness of the rhetorical structure of ideological discourse is advocated. The crux of Althusserian ideology theory, on the other hand, lies in the spelling out of the conveyance of dominant values through the variety of the so-called 'ideological apparatuses'.

The foregoing analysis of the relations between interest, power and legitimacy forces us to question the main assumptions of both these theoretical trends. The semiotics of ideology focuses on a real and fascinating dimension but it begins by *assuming* that ideology is primarily a 'sentiment' defined quite apart from any detailed social configuration of interest and power; belief is, once again, taken for granted; and so it is—even more—in the dogmatic stiffness with which Althusser decrees that his ideological apparatuses inculcate dominant creeds in everybody's minds in a truly one-way fashion. This time, however, in a de rigueur compliment to Marxism's proverbial power-mindedness, belief is an a priori conflated with power: *power pervades society in the guise of inculcated belief*. If one is naïve enough to ask how and why, one gets a ready (if over-hackneyed) answer: by means of the several ideological apparatuses (church, school, family, etc.) through which capitalists exploit the brains of working people. . . .

From the standpoint of the history of sociological theory, this is ludicrously ironical: for precisely when theorists gave up en masse the structural-functionalist view of role and internalization and became aware of its unacceptable holistic oversocializing bias (see pp. 53–61), structural Marxism subscribed to a rigid conception of role and of internalization. . . . Not surprisingly, Althusser defines ideology as a property of the social system, *not* of classes (and then, of course, proceeds to a sleight of hand, merely verbal identification of the social system with class domination). Thus dogmatic Marxism takes over from dogmatic functionalism (Althusser being no more than a deceptively tough-tongued Parsons), and we are back to the untenable niceties of the holistic concept of ideology.

I hope I have made clear that an analytically fruitful, truly operative theory of ideology can and must start from a much less far-fetched standpoint. Indeed, its first promise need not go beyond admitting that 'every established order tends to produce . . . the naturalization of its own arbitrariness', and that the main mechanism involved in the process is a subtle play of often unspoken assumptions governing 'the dialectic of objective chances and individual or group aspirations, out of which there develops a 'sense of limits' capable of being mistaken for the sense of reality itself'.[79] In his seminal work-in-progress on the sociology of habitus, Pierre Bourdieu calls the experience of such process *doxa*, 'so as to distinguish it from an orthodox or heterodox belief implying awareness and recognition of the possibility of different or antagonistic beliefs'.[80] It goes without saying that, while my theoretical path differs considerably from Bourdieu's, one chief advantage of the concept of ideology as power lies precisely in its ability to keep alive to the hidden, pervasive presence of doxa in the actual life of society. Moreover, the view of the habitus as a 'subjective, but not individual system of internalized structures, schemes of perception, conception and action common to all members of the same group or class'[81] rightly stresses internalization *within* class—not, as does Althusser, as a mysterious fluid inculcating power under the guise of belief and working from ruling to ruled groups.

Finally, a word about value-orientations as the embodiment of ideology as legitimacy. We saw how crucial the concept of value-orientation as 'the most general statements of *legitimate* ends which guide social action' is to a certain conception of legitimacy, basically associated with theorists like Parsons, Kluckhohn, Smelser and Deutsch. The interrelations between legitimacy, value-orientations and social symbolism represent for this school of thought the kernel of ideology. Legitimacy is here, first and foremost, an effect produced by the linking of any given experience with symbols carrying authority due to their embodiment of core values in a given culture.

The present analysis of the notion of ideology does not refuse in totum this understanding of the nexus between ideology and legitimacy. However, it utterly rejects its holistic framework. The sectional, class nature of ideological belief, its rooting on power-ridden situations, drastically minimizes the scope of unanimously held core values. It is only *within* each one of the ideological sets of a given society that the principle of legitimacy works as a cluster of value-orientations and effectively tends to confer validity on experiences by relating them to authoritative symbols bearing the main values of a social group. In other words, the objective correlative of value-orientations is class, not 'society'. Accordingly, the functionalist view of ideology as legitimacy is valid only as an internal dimension of the ideology-as-power perspective, not as an alternative to it. As a general theory, the recognition of legitimacy as ideology clearly prevails over the holistic naïveties of the ideology-as-legitimacy view.

(1977)

2   Remarks on the theory of culture

1 From historicism to anthropology

The task of conceptualizing culture may very easily turn into a
Herculean labour—or rather, a Sisyphean one; but the impressive
plethora of definitions, as in Kroeber and Kluckhohn's well-known
digest,[1] is to a considerable extent misleading, in so far as most of
the scholarly notions are either overlapping or tautological. At any
rate, a similar enterprise would be quite superfluous for our
purpose: for we scarcely need discuss the culture concept except for
the benefit of our views on the *sociology* of culture—an area of
study which we should avoid characterizing too much in abstracto.
I shall therefore restrict myself to highlighting and assessing four
main meanings of the term: the humanistic, the historicist-
anthropological, the structural-functionalist and the psycho-
analytical. The first two will be dealt with in the present section; the
latter two, in the final part of this chapter.

The handiest, as well as oldest, semantic level in the word culture
is still what deserves historically to be called its *humanistic*
meaning. By that I mean 'culture' in the intellectual, chiefly
educational, vaguely perfective, and above all *evaluative* sense of
the word—the sense we have in mind when we speak of a
'cultivated woman', or, then, of Paris as a living, and Alexandria
as a dead, 'centre of culture', and whose illustrious ancestry dates
back to the Hellenistic *paideia* and the dawn of the cult of
humanitas in the circle of Scipio Aemilianus. Three generations
after Scipio, the eclectic philosophy of Cicero secured the

definitive establishment of humanitas among the most cherished ideals of the West. Cicero was wont to translate paideia both as 'cultura animi' and as 'humanitas',[2] thus underlining its *personal* and *perfective* as well as its cosmopolitan and evaluative overtones.

The humanistic concept of culture long survived antiquity, in the spirit of that celebrated 'classical heritage'[3] which eventually became so petrified as to incense Nietzsche in his passionate craving for the (re)vitalization of culture. However, as classical humanism reached its last productive spell, in the age of Winckelmann and Goethe, another intellectual trend was gaining momentum in the very birthplace of neo-Hellenism, Germany. It came to be known as historicism.[4]

In Anglo-Saxon usage, thanks to Sir Karl Popper, 'historicism' came to mean chiefly 'an approach to the social sciences which assumes that *historical prediction* is their principal aim' (*The Poverty of Historicism*, 1957, p. 3). Conceived in this fashion, and broadly identified with Hegelian or Marxist philosophy of history, historicism bore the brunt of Popper's devastating onslaught—an attack, incidentally, basically akin to other, contemporary critiques of the fallacy of historical inevitability, the most famous of which is by far Sir Isaiah Berlin's Auguste Comte lecture delivered at the London School of Economics in 1953.

The historicism of our concern, however, is quite another matter. It is just an epistemological, not a 'prophetic', cast of mind, one of its most conspicuous features being precisely its resolute *avoidance* of historical prediction. 'The essence of historicism', wrote Meinecke, in what remains to date the standard study of the subject, 'is the substitution of a process of *individualizing* observation for a *generalizing* view of human forces in history.' Such a craze for the unique could never have stemmed from Hegel, who cherished the individual in history only in so far as it was the 'concrete universal', i.e. the embodiment of a general logos. As a matter of fact, Historismus did not descend from post-Kantian idealist metaphysics, but from Herder and from romantic or late-romantic historians like Ranke and Droysen.

The business of Historismus is the monographic grasping of historical individuality—a far remove from the sweeping generalizations of evolutionist philosophy of history. Ranke went as far as to protest against every attempt to subsume historical reality under any general concepts whatsoever, although, quite understandably, he himself was the first to sin against such a Procrustean precept in his own work. Even when not so radical, however, the historicists never tired of pursuing the historical object in its most peculiar, idiosyncratic aspects.

Historicism in this sense, it goes without saying, has no derogatory ring about it. Recently, however, the *pejorative* acceptance of the word has been considerably reinforced by dint of Althusser's 'structural' Marxism. Althusserians present themselves as fierce anti-Hegelians but they tend to lump both Hegelianism and Historismus together in abomination. Unfortunately, as the late George Lichtheim so shrewdly remarked, the Althusserian contempt for historicisms of all kinds actually serves as a rather tedious alibi for avoiding the pains of doing any empirical historical analysis at all—and very fortunately, we need not for our purpose go into details about neo-Marxist scholasticism.

On the other hand, the non-derogatory concept of historicism has been of late adopted by a major Anglo-Saxon historiographic endeavour, Donald Kelley's *Foundations of Modern Historical Scholarship* (1970). At the outset of his book, Professor Kelley describes historicism as the search not for the typical but for the unique in history—a change-minded quest that 'emphasizes the variety rather than the uniformity of human nature', and is interested 'less in similarities than in differences' (p. 4). Meinecke would find no difficulty in underwriting such a definition.

Now, *this* kind of historicism was precisely what gave rise to our second meaning of culture—the 'Teuto-anthropological' one.

The new sense of culture arose from a seminal change in an until then basic trait of the word: its synonymity with 'civilization'. Roughly speaking, up to Herder, culture and civilization alike denoted a progressive quality of both the material and the moral states of mankind as a whole. It took a protracted polemic of the German late eighteenth-century intelligentsia against their Frenchified courts to separate their meanings.[5] German bourgeois intellectuals, more often stemming from the lower middle class, began to *oppose* the spiritual authenticity of national Kultur to the *court*oisie, the cosmopolitan good manners inherent in post-baroque civilization—a concept where the two Voltairean values of the useful and the pleasant went hand in hand, an exquisite combination of comfort with charm. Little by little this socially motivated cultural revolt, dictated by a conspicuous need for self-legitimation, adopted a national ideology. Towards the end of Weimar classicism, the particularistic concept of culture was already firmly established. Although Weimar's cultural theorist par excellence, the great Wilhelm von Humboldt, stuck to the old sense of the term, Goethe came to speak of culture as an ensemble of knowledge, customs and traditions characteristic of a certain people. One can see how easily such a conception turned into a catchword for the nationalistic dramatization performed by Fichte's patriotic speeches and the romantics' love for the 'national' past; but long before romanticism, the highly influential thought of Herder had sealed the fate of Kultur through the emphasis he lent to the feeling of belongingness to a cultural group and the idea of the incommensurability of different cultural wholes.[6]

As a consequence, there evolved a lingering antithesis between civilization and culture in social thinking. Put in a nutshell, it amounts to the following:

(a) 'civilization', a mainly French and English usage, denotes a *universal*, eminently *transferable*, process of growing mastery over matter and barbarism, stressing human *capabilities* rather than specific works;
(b) 'culture', by contrast, chiefly a German acceptation, refers to a *particular* pattern of life, ultimately unimportable, with a focus on specific 'meaningful' historical *products* rather than on general capabilities.

The contrast is vividly expressed, in early twentieth-century social theory, in several French and German authors. Thus, while a Marcel Mauss reserves the name of 'phénomènes de civilisation' for the aspects of society that 'lend themselves naturally to diffusion', Alfred Weber sharply severs the 'cosmos of civilization', centring around science and technology, from the 'cosmos of culture', where man, no longer a discoverer of truth, but a creator of values, indulges in religion, philosophy and art. In the First World War, Western democracies stood for 'civilization', whereas Germany (including the young Thomas Mann) rose in defence of Kultur.[7]

Now this Teutonic concept of culture paved the way for the emergence of the anthropological sense of the word. To begin with, German historicism put aside the personal, perfective connotations of humanistic culture. The latter remained cherished, from Humboldt through Burckhardt up to Jaeger, as Bildung; but Kultur referred to a quite different thing. Historicist culture was *collective* instead of personal, *expressive* instead of perfective, *transmissible,* but *intransferable*, and empirically given instead of ideal-normative.

Moreover, in the end, historicism also did away with the *evaluative* dimension of the humanistic culture concept. Of course, eighteenth-century German historicism, in its obsession with ethnic authenticity, evinced a strong evaluative bias. Herder's tirades against French civilization did not rest only on a belief in the *equality* of the two national cultures; it expressed an almost hysterical sense of the *superiority* of German folk 'honesty' over French frivolous civility. The pre-romantic culture of the 'soul' did not aim solely at proving itself an equal to the neoclassic civilization of 'esprit'—it considered itself from the start as a healthy alternative to a sick, decadent way of life. At the same time, however, in terms of formal models of philosophical history, Herder's main achievement consisted in applying the *circular* pattern of history, from the salubrity of primitivisms to the disease of decadences, discerned by Winckelmann in ancient art, to the life-span of each national culture;[8] and in the long run, the levelling implications of such a cyclic view prevailed over the original value-laden propensity of historicism. After all, ethnic pride apart, German folk ethos could be deemed superior to French mores not as much because of racial supremacy as of evolutionary stage: allegedly (and rather whimsically) Germans were said to be in their primitive puberty, whereas France was thought to be living an end of cycle, a decrepit old age. As a piece of historiographical accuracy, this amounted to no more than rubbish; but as mythical idée-force, it contributed a powerful prop to the birth of a *neutral* and *pluralistic*, instead of *evaluative* and *universalistic*, idea of culture.

Above all, 'culture' became a plural noun. Humanistic paideia was essentially single, a formative process which, in its universalistic bent, prided itself in the unity of educated mankind against the congerie of barbaric customs. From the Stoic accent on cosmopolitan values down to Goethe's coinage of a concept like Weltliteratur, this sense of cultural unitarianism was a watermark of humanism. By contrast, historicism could only conceive of culture*s*, in the plural; in the singular, culture was always, to a historicist mind, preceded by an indefinite article emphasizing the plurality, the essential diversity of cultures along ethnic lines. As Bauman[9] puts it, a singular, *hierarchical* idea of culture gave way to an essentially plural, *differential* one. The sense of superiority in *unitarianism* began to be challenged by an egalitarian awareness of *uniqueness*. The chief responsible for this revolutionary intellectual shift was Herder. In fact, he insisted relentlessly on the equality of all cultures, however incommensurable; he might well have said of cultures what Ranke was later to assert of ages: that they are all 'unmittelbar zu Gott'. Thus the pluralistic neutrality vis-à-vis cultural particularism, professed by the historicist mind, heralded that 'de-evaluativization' of the culture concept, without which anthropology, as an empirical social science, could not have been born.

Herderian historicism is not unanimously accepted as the philosophical fountainhead, however indirect, of the pluralistic anthropological concept of culture. Bauman, for one, does not mention Herder and prefers to credit the Lockean critique of innatism with the undermining of the humanistico-hierarchical model;[10] but he also underlines the German philosophical upbringing of Malinowski, by far the most influential defender of the empathic grasping of cultural uniqueness through apprehending native Weltanschauungen and Volksgeisten.[11] Now this Diltheyan element in Malinowski derives from the great historicist tradition launched in the late eighteenth-century and handed down, via Schleiermacher's romantic hermeneutics, to Dilthey's fin-de-siècle neo-idealism. Besides, early modern anthropology's most distinctive mood was cultural relativism; and who else but Herder qualifies as the chief creator of the belief that human variety is bound to exist and is in itself an invaluable thing? Herder turned the expressiveness of nationhood, instead of the perfectibility of the individual, into the core of culture.

On the other hand, I see no contradiction in positing Locke's empiricism as a general pre-condition of a pluralist approach to culture, at the same time fully recognizing historicism as the principal originator of anti-ethnocentricity—the drive most naturally identified with the ethos of anthropology.

Historicism was also—much more than empiricism—the cradle of another basic tenet of the twentieth-century study of man: the idea of *concrete, richly determinate sociability*. As Sir Isaiah Berlin said,[12] the social nature of man had been invariably stated, from Aristotle and Aquinas to Grotius and Locke; but it had been asserted in all too general, abstract terms. It fell to Herder to fill the concept of human association with the teeming particularities that only historians used as yet to portray (and then, without, as a rule, bringing the zoon politikon theme under focus).

Again, this *specification* of man's social nature—what we might call the protosociology of historicism—was bequeathed by Herder to both Hegel and the anti-Hegelian romantics of the 'historical school' (Savigny, etc.). Translating Herder's populism into a conservatism inherited from Burke's praise of tradition and the social bond, German romantic legal thought was to follow a tack basically similar to French Restoration conservatism, also powerfully influenced by Burke. French legitimism was in turn a major formative component of the thinking of Saint-Simon and his disciple, that hidden romantic, Auguste Comte. Tracing his intellectual development, Comte himself described his 'doctrine sociale' as a synthesis of Condorcet's sketch of the progress of the mind through civilization and de Bonald's regressive royalism; he prided himself in having learned 'social dynamics'—the science of progress—from the Enlightenment philosophers, but 'social statics'—the science of order—from Restoration reactionary thinking. Later in the century, the same deep affection for supra-individualistic 'cakes of custom' reappeared in the sociolatry of the main theoretical source of both Malinowski and Radcliffe-Brown: Durkheim.

Moreover, historicism harbingered also what would be for long the most typical note of cultural anthropology: its insistence on the *pattern* of culture. The Herderian idea of culture as an integrated whole—a Gestalt—received a significant impulse, as Barbu[13] pointed out, in the studies of cultural *style*. Typified by Wölfflin's Kunstgeschichte, the use of stylistic concepts to denote a whole body of similarities and convergences in the cultural manifestations of a community triumphed with Nietzsche's momentous dichotomy of the Dionysian and the Appolonian, which directly inspired Ruth Benedict's *Patterns of Culture*. 'Style' and 'pattern'—the new magic words—were used interchangeably by Benedict, whose mentor, the linguist-anthropologist, Sapir, like herself a very gifted artistic personality, thought of culture in exceedingly aesthetic terms.

With regard to patterned culture, incidentally, the line that goes from Herder to early modern anthropology distinctly overarches Victorian ethnological theory. Indeed, what Marett termed 'Mr Tylor's science' set no great store by individual patterns of culture. True, *Primitive Culture* opened with a comprehensive definition of

45

culture as a 'complex whole'; but this did not prevent Tylor from specifying that the latter was taken 'in its wide ethnographic sense', with an accent more on 'wide' than on ethnographic. In fact, 'whole' was meant in terms strikingly similar to the as yet living meaning of good old 'civilization': not only does Tylor begin his famous definition by a characteristic 'culture *or civilization*', but he stresses what we feel tempted to call the *competence* aspect of culture: '. . . that complex whole which includes knowledge, belief, art, morals, law, custom, *and any other capabilities* and habits acquired by man as a member of society'.[14] Terminologically and conceptually alike, the father of cultural anthropology is closer to 'civilization' than to 'Kultur' semantics—certainly closer to Mauss than to Alfred Weber. After all, Tylor's point was to demonstrate 'the uniformity which so largely pervades civilization'; hence his seeing culture, 'complex whole' or not, as a general 'condition' and not a pattern—a suitable subject for 'the study of laws of human thought and action[15] rather than for the idiographic methods subsequently adopted by cultural anthropologists.[16]

Enfin Kroeber vint. He confirmed and refined the Teuto-anthropological concept, underlining its pluralistic and holistic overtones, but his major contribution, as is well known, lies in the introduction of the 'superorganic' (a borrow from Spencer) nature of culture thesis. Kroeber proposed to see culture as a 'coral reef' of artifacts, customs and ideas, the product of endless secretions deposited by organic, individual polyps, and yet outliving them all, besides giving each of them an indispensable base for their own limited survival. Unlike the reef, however, culture was also seen as *normative*—or as a reef, determining not only *that*, and where, its polyps live, but also *how* they do.[17] This emphasis on normativeness was basically alien to the historicist legacy, and so it was Kroeber's awareness of the compositeness of culture, due to diffusion,[18] but reinforced by the importance of cross-cultural systemic patterns[19] and of the presence of sub-cultures related to social stratification[20]—all of which shows that Kroeber modulated the historicist heritage, which reached him considerably modified by the moderate diffusionism of his teacher Boas.

Superorganicism has been hotly debated. Some greeted it as a wholesome reaction against Boas's inhibitory particularism, and as such, the seminal, if paradoxical, source of White's materialistic 'cultorology', with its vindication of universal, energy-conditioned evolution.[21] Others (notably Bidney) sternly rebuked Kroeber for hypostatizing culture, accused superorganicism of idealism and proposed to replace it by a rather clumsy 'psycho-cultural' approach.[22] Since the beginning of the 1960s, there arose a more serious line of attack. Physical anthropology, placing the hunting, erect and faber, and yet small-brained Australopithecine fossils from the upper Pliocene and lower Pleistocene among the hominids, much discredited one of the basic tenets of the superorganicists: their postulation of a sudden, all-or-none appearance of culture.[23] We must now study hominization within the broad framework of cynegetization of primates; we ought, in Moscovici's pithy sentence, to focus on 'le devenir homme du chasseur', no longer on 'le devenir chasseur de l'homme'.[24]

However, superorganicism, I surmise, is not entirely destroyed by the new findings of physical anthropology. One can very well drop the 'critical point theory of the appearance of culture' (Geertz) and yet stick to the superorganic theory of culture in so far as the latter is the product of *emergent evolution*. If we look at the matter with the eyes of Sir Karl Popper's later writings, and see Kroeber's 'coral reef' as the result of the vast Darwinian affair of life as an continuing problem-solving affair, then the superorganic, in its primal sense of something irreducible to either the physical or the psychic reality of its bearers—the succession of men throughout history—is indeed vindicated as Popper's 'world 3': the (partially) autonomous world of thought contents viewed in themselves, as opposed to the world of things and that of thought processes.[25]

In his recent intellectual autobiography, Popper proposes to include in world 3 'all the products of the human mind, such as tools, institutions and works of art'. He regards the mind, endowed with a genetically given capacity for *descriptive* language (itself the root of the power of imagination), as an organ that creates objects of world 3 and interacts with them.[26] Descriptive language unfolds in history as the great inborn prop of '*exosomatic* evolution'[27] The similarity with the Kroeberian concept of culture, taken at its global and macro-historical level, is quite striking.

On the other hand, Popper's insistence on the crucial role of *descriptive* language in emergent evolution qualifies very opportunely one of the major weaknesses in the 'critical-point' theory about the rise of culture: its jealous assertion of a human monopoly of language. Monopoly there is; but only of the *upper potentialities* of language, not of the latter as a general communicative function, since the homo loquens—any more than faber, or socius—can no longer see himself as the only species possessing such faculties.

So much for superorganicism. Unlike Bauman, who thinks it implies a 'vexing dilemma' as regards the existential status of culture,[28] I tend to believe that Kroeber's central views hold good enough; but this is, of course, the superorganic in as much as it refers to the biological level. Whenever Kroeber got into the particularization of culture—that is, whenever he left the conceptualization of culture as a human condition and came to the study of the generalities of *situated* cultures—he often lapsed into the worst foibles of historicist culturalism. For instance, he stressed, rather uncritically, cultural integration and value-sharing, and sought 'total-culture patterns' by means of an unabashedly psychologistic concept of ethos.[29] In the last analysis, he was a configurationalist through and through, a proponent of an 'artistic' hermeneutics as the method for grasping the inner sense of cultural wholes, who extolled rather uncritically the full-fledged psychologism of Benedict. Unfortunately, it was not only in the willingness to break the ascetic theoretical diet of field-workism that Kroeber departed from Boasian morphologism. The main drive of his theorizing also moved away from Boas in another, far less felicitous, respect: it exchanged the rigours of empirical-mindedness for a doubtful, intuitivistic psychologism—one definitely closer to the father of configurationalism, Frobenius, than to Boas. Nor did he demur at opposing 'history' to 'science'.[30] In a deep sense, Kroeber made cultural anthropology an heir to German historicism and its romantic ingredients.

Kroeber's towering summa helped more than anything to enthrone the concept of culture, anthropology's 'greatest contribution to the social sciences'.[31] Once freed from historicist metaphysics and romantic epistemology, such a concept presents obvious operational advantages vis-à-vis its humanistic pedagogic predecessor. The anthropological notion of culture is much wider in scope than the old ethico-educational one. In Kroeber, it explicitly embraced both material and non-material culture (though the difference was downgraded as of mere 'practical convenience'.[32] Linton gave material culture an important place in his distinction between the *use* (relation of a culture trait or complex to reality *outside* the society and culture) and the *function* (relation *within* the society and culture) of cultural units or wholes.[33] Wissler's rather confused 'universal culture pattern' comprehended nine orbits, including 'material traits' (the economy and weaponry) and 'knowledge' (myth as well as science).[34] Finally, Malinowski, in his article on culture for the *Encyclopaedia of the Social Sciences*, stated that culture comprises 'artifacts, goods, technical processes, ideas, habits and values'—as broad a range as Tylor's.[35]

Ten years later, while distinguishing between a 'material' and a 'spiritual' culture, the former composed of the social habits and institutions, the latter of the beliefs, ideas and values held in common by the members of a society, he invited anthropologists to see culture as a set of basic 'functional imperatives' met by institutionalized mechanisms of response. Thus economic life was a response to the imperative of production and reproduction of the apparatus of implements and goods; social control, a response to the need for regulation of behaviour; the educational system, the fulfilment of renewal and training of the human material allocated to the several institutions in society and political organization, a response to the imperative of defining authority and providing it with a power machinery.[36]

As Parsons himself was quick to notice, this declension of culture into functional imperatives closely resembled his own 'social system', refurbished, a little after the book of that name, in the so-called AGIL scheme, where the functions of environmental adaptation (A), goal-attainment (G), integration (I) and latency or pattern-maintenance (L) are carried out by four sub-systems of society: the economy, the polity, the societal community and the culture.[37]

Briefly speaking, then, Malinowski's last conceptualization of culture was so wide as to encompass the social structure and, in reality, become the equivalent of the social system as a whole. The truth is that such a broad picture of culture, if it did not impair the meticulous Malinowskian ethnography of very small Oceanic societies, could scarcely serve—any more, for that matter, than Parsons's AGIL model—as an operational device to *explain* any specific dimension of social life. Today it is common knowledge that Malinowski never actually portrayed any culture in its full entirety (How could he, or anyone else?), and that the holism of his view of culture boiled down in practice to something humbler, but admirably well-done: the description of one or *some* institutions against a skilfully drawn background composed of the remaining traits or patterns. However necessarily incomplete, competent field-work in manageable culture areas could support the illusion of grasping culture wholes.

In their ethnographic activity, then, anthropologists assumed that culture consisted just of *learned behaviour socially transmitted*. However, to this bare and basic assumption they used to add three presuppositions:

(a) (tribal) culture was tacitly identified with shared *uniform* behaviour, descriptively derived from alleged averages of conduct in sex, age and occupation roles said to obtain in self-contained, homogeneous societies;

(b) this assumed uniform behaviour was in turn identified with a *culture pattern*, that is, an underlying unity and consistency (the only difference was, it seems, that holism became in British anthropology an image of 'social structure', that is to say, of a set of interweaving *roles,* whilst in American anthropology, holism turned out a picture of 'culture' proper, meaning a well-knit set of *norms and values*); and

(c) culture patterns were seen as essentially discrete, i.e. in contrast with every other, so that culture-pattern theorists subscribed, explicitly or implicitly, to a full-blown *cultural relativism*.

Steward[38] sensibly singled out the inadequacy of such premises as soon as the anthropologist turns to complex societies, where culture very seldom evinces behavioural uniformity, cultural integration is generally *not* achieved through sameness of individual conduct (thereby denying any visible compact pattern) and, last but not least, both socialization and enculturation tend to be modulated along varying, often conflicting, loci of social structure.

Besides, by the time White and Steward attempted to re-weld evolution and culture, the most provocative among theoretical developments in the discipline—the then nascent so-called structural anthropology—was denying the existence of patterns even in 'primitive' culture. Thus, after having stressed that the several symbolic systems in any given society are 'incommensurable'[39] Lévi-Strauss linked the occurrence of historical change (diachrony) in primitive social systems to the tensional dynamics inherent in the relations between 'structures of communication' and those of 'subordination'.[40] This was surely no return to the Boasian 'shreds-and-patches' image of culture—but neither was it anything close to the myth of compact cultural consistency indulged in by most anthropologists of both functionalist and configurationalist persuasions. A firm believer in social entropy (so much so, that he cherishes the pun 'structural entropology'), Lévi-Strauss brushed 'pattern' aside as a typical functionalist fallacy.

Indeed, like Malinowski's holism, the postulates of pattern and cultural relativism à outrance were very much 'optical illusions' encouraged by the contingencies of the terrain. Just as the Malinowskian ideal of ethnographic thoroughness seemed feasible as long as field-work concentrated on his thin Polynesian tribes (but became increasingly problematical as soon as anthropologists started to apply the technique of participant observation to large-scale African societies), so the functionalist belief in the compact pattern of isolated, autarkical cultures hinged to a great extent on the strictly *temporary* circumstance that the British Empire provided its anthropologists with field-work subjects as yet remote enough from modernizing forces as to spare such cultures (African or Oceanic) the higher degrees of deculturation other primitive societies (like the American Plains Indians) already had to go through.[41]

As for the third sin of yesterday's anthropological culture theory, namely, cultural relativism, it has been still more shaken than the myth of pattern by structural anthropology. The days when a Sapir rebuked a Lowie for his temerity in mentioning 'universals of the mind' belong to a distant past. If there is one central problématique Lévi-Strauss raised cogently anew, that is the nature of human *universals*. Following some perceptive recent analyses,[42] we may venture to assert that Lévi-Strauss succeeded in re-thinking the problem of anthropology as the study *of man* (and not only of cultures) because he refused to answer an intractable poser: Where are the universals in culture to be located? In the endless cultural variations of common traits or in the common denominators themselves? Pursuing the universal in the variations of cultural traits, one invariably runs the risk of losing sight of universality. On the other hand, sticking to a handful of 'common denominators', one gets nothing more than vapid generalities, and, worse still, 'fake universals' (Kroeber). The great merit of Lévi-Strauss lies in his understanding that cultural variations are but the raw material of anthropology, its real object being the systematic character underneath *their very variability*. Instead of listing flat, uninteresting common traits, structural anthropology set out to look for the fascinating mechanisms of their transformations. A quest for identity through the discovery of differences—such is the path opened by structuralist to the science of man.

The structuring power of human mind, the Lévi-Straussan 'esprit' as an active grid, an ubiquitous structura structurans shaping (though not in the least creating) human experience and social life, is in effect neither a contingent manifestation of any particular culture, nor an obvious, empty commonality (though it still suffers, in Sperber's opinion, from a minimalist view of human nature, one that does not justice to its full richness). A kind of deep grammar of culture, the mind-as-grid hypothesis even revolutionizes the traditional idea of the relation between the innate and the learned or acquired in human behaviour.

More specifically, structuralism supersedes the tendency to regard as innate only attributes *in opposition* to those acquired; it invites us to distinguish the learned elements from shaping, ordering apparatuses which, though themselves undoubtedly 'learned' by the species at a given point in history, play nevertheless the role of innate devices in the culture-differentiating process.[43] The seminal value of such a perspective scarcely needs emphasizing.

Malinowski's biologistic theory of drives, with its mixture of common-sense triviality and arbitrariness, was one of the weakest points in his theorizing, nearly endangering the legitimacy of the quest for cultural universals. Structural anthropology restored to the latter its intellectual dignity and creativity. The same could be said of Clifford Geertz's parallel views about culture as a 'control mechanism': culture seen not as complexes of concrete behaviour patterns but as a set of behaviour *programmes*, of capabilities for the governance of conduct, whose 'dialogue' with environmental conditions would in principle explain the narrowing of man's largely indeterminate potential into the specifics of his actual achievements.[44] Geertz is, for that matter, clearly echoing the structuralist computer-like concern with a generalized 'logic of the concrete' when he urges anthropologists in search of universals 'to look for systematic relationships among diverse phenomena, not for substantive identities among similar ones'.[45]

It goes without saying that a historical-minded sociology of culture, focusing on 'hot' societies, would scarcely be able to rely on a culture concept tallying with the standard functionalist assumption of behavioural consensus, compact consistency and cultural idiosyncratic insularity. The cultural field with which, as can easily be imagined, such a historical study deals—complex social formations on a larger-than-national scale—hardly yields to such holistic biases.

Before taking leave of the culture concept, however, we must turn briefly to the special inflexion its holistic version received in functionalist *sociological* theory.

2 The oversocialized conception of culture

When historicism did away with the normative, pedagogic concept of culture, it also cast a shadow on one important aspect of the humanist idea: its concern with humanity as a function of the individual person. The living subject of paideia, humanitas, or Bildung was in effect always an individual; but in the holism inherent in the historicist culture concept, the notion of culture as an individual attribute scarcely survived.

It is not that historicist historians and their unwitting intellectual kinsmen, holist anthropologists, dislike individuality. On the contrary, as we have seen, they profess a sincere fondness of historical or cultural uniqueness; but mark: the individuals they so respect and exalt, jealously guarding them against subsumption under the typical or general, are always *collective wholes*. True historicist historians have more often than not little love for the socially divisive potential of class and personality; they think in terms of nations and ages, never of persons and classes. (When they do, like the individualist Carlyle or the populist Michelet, they become spurious historicists: historicists with a strong tendency to collapse into the generalities of philosophy of history, the bête noire of genuine historicists.) As for holist anthropologists, have they not been justly considered liberals in their own society but stubborn Tories in the societies they study? Historicists may like individuality; yet, as good holists, they feel no affection towards *individualism*.

The business of the present section, where, by assessing two more meanings of culture—the structural-functionalist and the psycho-analytical—we shall close our remarks on the theory of culture, is to show how questionable is this anti-individualism ethos, bequeathed by historicism to social theory. When I say question-able I mean that the anti-individualism of holism is criticizable on sound *theoretical* grounds, not just on moral ones. It is not our liberalism that rejects it; it is social theory itself.

The epitome of the anti-individualistic bent of the anthropo-sociological culture concept lies in the late Talcott Parsons's view of culture. His conception of culture as the social sub-system in charge of 'latency', i.e. of motivational inputs, has already been referred to. For Parsons, culture ensures that deep internalization of norms without which the integrity of the 'societal community' would be imperiled. One distinctive feature of his social thought is its blending of the Durkheimian theme of the integrative effects of coercive social norms with Mead's insights on internalization devices (such as the 'generalized other' image) and Linton's theory of role (whose own starting-point is, of course, Mead's homonymous concept).

Parsons's own internalization theory claims to be a 'Freudianiz-ation' of Mead's social psychology. It attaches great importance to Freud's superego, the agency of internalization of moral standards; but for Parsons, what is internalized are not only moral norms but cognitive categories and expressive symbols as well. Besides, the adventurous Meadian self, always going to and fro between its Jamesian poles, the autonomous 'I' and the socially shaped 'me', becomes a personality much more moulded by society. All in all, Mead's original perspective was in several major points rather the opposite of the structural-functionalist one: it refused to conceive of social action as an emanation of societal structure, denied the reduction of social interaction to interaction between social roles, and challenged the idea that society is held together by its members' sharing of common values.[46]

However, the Parsonian 'Freudianization' of Mead is only a step towards a thorough-going *Durkheimianization of Freud*. Among Parsons's chief aims there lies the wish to make Durkheim and Freud complementary to each other. In his essay 'The superego and the theory of social systems', he notices that Durkheim fails to recognize that the social system hinges on the interaction of personalities, whereas Freud missed the systemic nature of individuals' interactions.[47]

But the alleged 'complementarity' between Durkheim and Freud is deceptive. Although Parsons is fully conscious that 'role-involvements do not exhaust the orientation or interest system of any personality',[48] this awareness does not produce the least analytical result. The whole tenor of his work displays a strong tendency to forget what Freud never forgot—yet what Dennis Wrong[49] had to remind structural-functionalists of: that man is a *social animal, but not an altogether socialized one.* (A few years later, Parsons became also the main target of *Homo Sociologicus*,[50] Ralf Dahrendorf's famous critique of the sociological reifying hypostasis of the role concept.) Even a critic as appreciative as Guy Rocher finds Parsons really guilty of having 'sociologisé la motivation de l'action'.[51]

Structural-functionalism is, indeed, of the 'two sociologies', the one which posits social norms as *constitutive*, rather than regulative, of the self; social actors (*qua* role bearers) as a reflex of the social system; and meaning, as a faithful imprint of the cultural pattern.[52] If, on the one hand, the integration of common values with the deeply internalized need-dispositions of the socii is for Parsons the 'core phenomenon' of social dynamics,[53] and, on the other hand, the very springs of action are reduced by his outright anti-instinctivism to *learned* dispositions shaped by the cultural system, then the motivational issue by which Parsons appears to be so beset—'the Hobbesian problem of order',[54] described by him as the fons et origo of the sociological quest—actually is no problem at all; it is rather a foregone conclusion. As Bocock remarks:[55] 'if, as Parsons thinks, there can *never* be an id-impulse as such for the individual, since it must always be seen as part of the expressive symbolism of a common culture', then it is very hard to conceive of the possibility of someone being in conflict with one's society: No room is left for the alas too frequent tensions the ego experiences when torn between its superego, (social) values and its own rebellious id-impulses.

Ironically enough, there existed a *genuine* Hobbesian problem of order underneath the empirical functionalism that preceded that of Parsons (and that he prided himself in having theoretically enlarged and refined). For Malinowski, man is as appetitive, as potentially aggressive an animal as Hobbes's homini lupus.[56] However debatable, at least Malinowski's instinctivism had the good sense to never lose sight altogether of the individual and his impulsive drives.

Understandably, British anthropological theorists like Firth and Nadel, who, in the 1950s, rebelled against Radcliffe-Brownian social-structuralism and claimed the need to take into account the ultimately irrepressible manipulative character of the individual and the fundamentally interest-driven nature of his behaviour, did not conceal their allegiance to Malinowki.[57] Nadel, for instance, rephrases and develops the Linton-Parsons role analysis so as to include a portrayal of manipulative traits of role expectancies[58]—a remarkable improvement on the Parsonian idealization (and not only stylization) of behavioural patterns. Nor is it hard to find the same strain of thought in the tradition of 'symbolic interactionism' and its legacy. In particular, Goffman's 'dramaturgical' view of ever precarious, often disrupted role performances dramatized also the self's social predicament; not suprisingly, his microsociological approach did not take long to turn to the study of deviance[59]—still one of the best correctives against any fetishism of the 'common culture'.

Long before modern social theory, however, the rights of the unsocializable side of man had achieved full recognition. In his essay, 'The natural principle of the political order', Kant tackled the problem most perceptively. Man, he wrote, has an inclination to socialize himself by associating with others, for only in such a condition can he best develop his natural capacities; notwithstanding, he has also a strong tendency to *individualize* himself in isolation from others. Such was the 'unsocial sociability' of man. Early modern radical political philosophy did not baulk at the problem. Rousseau, for one, knew that the institution of a just society demanded a wilful transformation of human nature that would change 'each individual, who is per se a perfect and solitary whole', into a part of a bigger whole whence he receives 'his nature and his being' (*Social Contract*, II, ch. 7).

More than a century later, Simmel, who attached great importance to Kant's remarks on 'unsocial sociability', echoed almost word for word Rousseau's realization that the relation between individual and society is to a large extent a necessarily tensional one. He saw society as a whole always trying to impose the one-sidedness of partial functions upon its members, whereas each of these strives on his part *to be also a whole*, not merely a one-sided part. 'No house can be built of houses, not only of specially formed stones', wrote Simmel in his beautifully aphoristic style. Society is precisely this 'impossible', no matter how necessary, house made of (refractory) houses.[60]

Durkheim never disguised the coercive power of the social norm. As Parsons himself observed,[61] he became increasingly obsessed by anomie—and passed his later years devising ideological compensations for the otherwise insufficient cohesiveness of that very organic solidarity he had previously found so much more integrative than the mechanical bounds of primitive society.

However, from beginning to end, he defined society not only by its externality but above all by its power to impose itself forcibly both on the individual behaviour and on the inner recesses of the individual mind.

In Parsons, by contrast, coerciveness tends to be somewhat played down, while a benignly harmonious collective assimilation of social rules and values is brought forward. Compared to the gloomy colours of Durkheim's view of social evolution, Parsonian Grand Theory displays from the start a serene confidence in norm-pervasiveness and long-run social stability. In point of fact, Parsons's systemic outlook is to a large extend Durkheim minus anomie—a subject that would have fallen in abeyance under the sway of structural-functionalism, were it not for the work of the nearly anti-systemic Merton.

All the same, like Parsons, Durkheim recognized the 'dualism of human nature'; he saw man, in his inmost being, torn between a purely individual life based on the organism and another, social existence, wholly identified with society.[62] Like the Christian moralists, however, he equated the first nature of this *homo duplex* with the world of appetite and sensation, reserving for his social personality the 'higher' spheres of thought and morality. By so doing, Durkheim prefigured the Parsonian tacit suppression of culture's partial rooting in the individual libido. Here, more than anywhere else, lies the hub of the deep convergence between the thought of Durkheim and that of Parsons—what Bauman sarcastically terms 'Durksonianism'.[63] Neither the founder of academic sociology nor the author of its most ambitious post-classical theoretical endeavour paid any attention to the profound insight of Diderot: just is the society where the law acknowledges the instincts.

Psychoanalysis did. If a man ever held true to this enlightened and libertarian (however utopian) dictum, that man was Sigmund Freud. As is widely known, he was very far from being a messianic dreamer; moreover, he expressly acknowledged the necessity of culture as a repressive force withstanding man's destructive impulses. Yet Freud never legitimized culture altogether, not even in this self-preserving human function. Being too much of a post-romantic to idealize, let alone sanctify, the realm of desire, he nevertheless refused to the end to accept any socially imposed *surplus* repression. His patron saints remained, throughout his life, not any jealous, overbearing god of coercive order imposing (as

Auden's beautiful epicedium has it) a repressive Generalized life, but the winged and sensuous, constructive and liberating deities of the will-to-pleasure:

One rational voice is dumb; over a grave
The household of Impulse mourns one dearly loved.
    Sad is Eros, builder of cities,
    And weeping anarchic Aphrodite.

In the Freudian image of culture, therefore, there is no such thing as a legitimate oversocialization of man.[64] To quote a balanced, far-sighted study in the interchange between psychoanalysis and sociology by the late Professor Roger Bastide: 'il y a seulement utilisation du social par le libidineux ou du libidineux par le social, passage d'un plan à l'autre, mais non identité de nature'.[65]

Indeed, classical psychoanalysis represents to my knowledge the best rejoinder to the holistic hypostatization of cultural uniformity, consistency and 'spirituality' perpetrated by sociological theory, be it classical or post-classical. That great and tragically neurotic scholar, Max Weber, once wrote that psychoanalysis could be the more useful the less it stuck to the secret 'libertinism' involved in the repression concept. How right he was in so viewing the nature of Freudian analytic—and yet how wrong in his evaluation of it! The only way psychoanalysis can be *centrally*, and not only peripherally, helpful to sociology depends precisely on its faithfulness to the irreducible libertarian aspects of the libido (in a sense, libertinism is libertarianism in morals). As Foucault[66] perceived, psychoanalysis of this sort is an indispensable 'counter-science'—a critical consciousness of social science; and Freudism in this connection is really Freud's one, not his disciples' elaborations or departures. For instance, Róheim's renowned thesis, where culture equals collective sublimation, a communal set of psychic defence mechanisms against anxieties,[67] may be surely insightful; and so is his stressing the culture-generative power of sublimation as distinct from neurosis (whereas neuroses separate, sublimations unite). Significantly, a recent effort to the effect of theoretically grounding a sociology of culture, Martindale's *Sociological Theory and the Problem of Values*, invites us to see culture, as 'a comprehensive system', in terms of 'symbolic closure' and sublimation, strikingly similar to Róheim's views.[68]

However, in our context, Róheim's psychosociology of sublimation clearly misses the point. More specifically, its legitimation of culture looks particularly one-sided, because unfaithful to the invaluable Freudian sense of the radical *ambiguity of culture*: positive culture is as a necessary containment of aggression, yet essentially illegitimate as the seat of social repression. Freud's uncomfortable *dual vision of culture* remains the sharpest reply to the quite repressive idea of a dualism of human nature. Besides, as an attempt at explanation, this part of classical psychoanalysis, for all its metapsychological ingredients, seems to me far more capable of qualifying as a fruitful metaphysical research programme[69] than its only serious competitor in the debunking of established culture, Nietzsche's 'genealogy of morals'. Sociology, as said the sociologist and distinguished interpreter of Freud, Philip Rieff, has not yet listened 'to what is *not* done, to the closed possibilities, to the . . . suppressed'[70]—and listen to it indeed it should.

'How is it that every society seems to get, more or less, the social character it "needs"?' Asking this question—a rephrasing, in the language of social psychology, of Parsons's Hobbesian problem of order—a quarter of a century ago, Riesman resorted to the cultural school of psychoanalysis and found his answer in Fromm: 'In order that any society may function well, its members must acquire the kind of character which makes them *want* to act in the way they *have* to act as members of the society or of a special class within it'.[71] Today, what seems attractive to us in Riesman's way of putting such a question is his mental restriction (piercing in that 'more or less') as to the integration of character and society, plus his visible scepticism towards the notion of social 'needs'.

Unfortunately, these healthy doubts as to the extent and legitimacy of the social moulding of the psyche, which lend Riesman's book (as well as the early Fromm's writings) a tantalizing ambivalence, were not to prevail. Shortly after the issue of *The Lonely Crowd*, the Parsonian reduction of self-gratifying impulses (cathexis) to the superior interests of society won the day. Despite some topical lip-service statements to the contrary, *within structural-functionalism, cathexis became libido, tamed by the raison de société*.

Thus Kluckhohn, in a typically Parsonian mood, demoted the cathectic in the name of value.[72] The disjunction between value and libidinal cathexis, the likelihood of decathected, ungratifying compliance with the social norm, cannot but embarass the Parsonian infatuation with shared values and systemic harmony. In fact, it is precisely this disjunction that arouses the human piety of

59

a critical sociology of culture—one that would put its pride, not on humanistic preaching, nor in the mirage of anthropomorphic knowledge, but in the silent unravelling of the many-armed threads of social repression.

We are now in a position to sum up the main steps in our review of the culture concept and its history. These steps have been as follows:

(a) The *historicist* appropriation of the idea of culture gave it a new range of meaning, much more comprehensive than its traditional humanistic acceptation. (Paraphrasing the original title of Carlo Antoni's seminal book, we labelled it 'from historicism to anthropology'.)

(b) Whilst *classical anthropology* confirmed this new scope, as well as the usage of culture as an expressive, instead of perfective, predicate of collectivities, rather than of individuals, modern anthropology, through the *superorganicist tenet*, achieved a reasonable demarcation of culture as mankind's status in the broad context among animal life.

(c) Subsequently, functionalist or configurationalist ethnography employed a particularistic concept of culture, which overstated its uniformity and consistency, even at primitive society level.

(d) The neo-evolutionist critique of functionalism, however, on the one hand, and the revival of interest in human universals fostered by the structural approach to kinship and myth, on the other, came to outline the relinquishment of holistic biases.

(e) Most unfortunately, the shortcomings of functionalist culturalism were strongly reinforced in the sociological theory prevalent until the 1960s by dint of Parson's oversocialized conception of man.

(f) It is suggested, however, that a fresh look at the psychoanalytic heuristics (as distinct from its rickety explanations) of the relations between impulse and norm virtually provides the sociology of culture with a more critical and realistic perspective.

This Freudian viewpoint is vital in that it helps shun one of the most fettering habits of holistic sociology of culture, to wit the tendency to exclusive concentration on *institutional* aspects, in socially accepted or required conduct and ideas. A sociology feeding on psychoanalysis seems uniquely able to explore the surreptitious underground of latent or censored social life, not a bit less significant, or decisive, than the Olympian order of sanctified norms, official mores and expected behaviour; otherwise, we would constantly run the risk of taking legitimacy essentially at its face value, and illegitimacy in its repressive, power-determined sense.

With the reference to the Freudian view of culture, our semantic survey reaches a kind of cyclic end; for, in a sense, Freud's awareness of the ambiguity of culture—his illuminating approach to the problem of cultural legitimacy—harks back to our first, pre-scientific meaning: the humanistic, self-perfective signification of 'culture'. With Freud, for the first time ever since the historicist 'collectivization' of the idea of culture, its bearing on individual life is assessed anew. At the same time, however, the extent to which the culture concept has become intrinsically problematic comes to the fore. In the first individual-minded meaning of culture, the latter was essentially a blissful gift to, as well as an extension of, personality. In the psychoanalytic image of culture, contrariwise, the individual has to defend himself against social culture—and vice versa. Culture, any more than individual impulse, is no longer a priori legitimate. The age of innocent cultural legitimacy is finished: the hour of (cultural) legitimacy *as a problem* has struck.

(1976)

3 Methodological infrastructuralism: an approach to the sociology of culture

Cultural subjects are getting an increasing appeal in sociological thinking. Some scholars even find that the main thrust of recent social theory springs just from the cultural domain.[1] However, there remain plenty of reasons to agree fully with Donald MacRae's warning, made less than a decade ago: 'The sociological theory of culture—at least as important as the theory of structure—hardly exists'.[2]

The main business of the present chapters is the assessment, no matter how brief, of the basic conceptual equipment of this sociological branch; and since we have already discussed, as it were, its subject-matter by examining the culture concept, we must now turn to its main epistemological and methodological aspects.

An approach to the sociology of culture

Theorists are quite aware of the basic interpenetration of culture and society. They know that the two are distinct only analytically, being actually inseparable, like the sides of a coin or, in Kroeber's famous analogy, the two faces of a sheet of paper. All the same, the distinction between the cultural, meaning a given set of socially held values and symbols, and the social (or, more precisely, the *societal*), indicating the system of interaction and stratification in a given society, enjoys the status of a 'major axis of sociological analysis'.[3] It is, however, a very tensional axis indeed. The history of social science is full of instances of both *culturalism*, the theoretical swallowing up of sociality by the cultural, and *sociologism*, the dissolution of culturality into the social.

Simmel's celebrated dictums to the effect that everything is 'sociation' were in this respect an unacknowledged prototype of Radcliffe-Brown's wilful denial of the legitimacy of a 'science of culture'.[4]

Against these examples of extreme sociologism, there stands an impressive array of once prestigious culturalisms. For a spell, Harvard sociology, the citadel of theory in American social science, was dominated by the rival culturalisms of Sorokin and Parsons. The former's vastly arbitrary classification of 'basic types' of culture ultimately traced them back to 'systems of truth' (ideational, idealistic, sensate) soaring high above the pedestrian details of social structure; his 'socio-cultural dynamics' was far more cultural than social.[5] As to Parsons, although he was to moderate considerably the downright idealism of his beginnings, he has remained a culturalist in the emphasis he puts on values as the patterning factor of social systems. Characteristically, the 'principal types of social structure' described in *The Social System* are distinguished in terms of prevalent 'value-orientations'. Moreover, in the cybernetic model of society and social evolution depicted by the later Parsons, the regulative role is consigned to the cultural system.[6]

We should be careful not to present sociologism and culturalism as *symmetric* opposites. The very formalism of Simmel's theoretical work denotes that he was not trying to reduce culture to society but rather to reduce sociology to the study of sociation patterns. This is sociologism by contraction, not by imperialistic expansion. Sorokin's 'sociocultural dynamics', on the contrary, is a clear-cut culturalist imperialism: it posits faith, value and belief as a prius to social structure; his is a spiritualistic organicism whose equals are not to be sought in sociology proper but in the philosophy of history of a Spengler or a Toynbee. Nevertheless, a sociology of culture worth its name can hardly be expected to ignore Radcliffe-Brown's wise warning: 'if you study culture, you are always studying the acts of behaviour of a specific set of persons who are linked together in a social structure'.[7] One may not be all the time focusing exactly on 'persons' (no matter their ontological status as 'bearers' of social reality), and yet—if one's aim is to give a sociological account of cultural phenomena—refer them to their social basis. Therefore, the first commandment of every sociology of culture ought to be an *anticulturalist caveat* (which does not in the least entail treating culture as a mere epiphenomenon of society).

More specifically, an anticulturalist strategy strives to avoid what Blake and Davis so aptly named 'the fallacy of normative determinism'[8]—the fallacy consisting in taking the fact that (value-loaded) norms are *meant* to control behaviour as the grounds for assuming that they actually fully *do*, thus falling into a highly unrealistic 'blueprint theory of society' (the kind of mirage in which social-action theorists like Parsons and Kluckhohn are prone to incur).

Normative determinism is unsatisfactory both on the descriptive and on the explanatory planes. Descriptively, its insufficiency has been summarized by Aberle.[9] The description of a language ensures our understanding of the content of verbal communication, yet does not by itself provide information about the network of communication; in much the same way, the systematic characteristics of a culture—its mode of relation with the environment, its way of linking the economy to the polity, etc.—do not emerge from any description of a given set of value-orientations. As for the explanatory flaws in normative culturalism, they amount to the following petitio principii: values, norms and motives are always *inferred* from observable behaviour, and therefore have no better claim to a causal status than the very phenomena from which they are inferred.[10] Inferring them is not epistemologically illicit; but to attach causal force to the inference is.

However, straightforward normativisms such as those of Parsons are far from being the only specimen of the culturalist illusion. On the contrary: *culturalism often speaks with an anticulturalist voice.* So, the more mistrustful our caveat the better: for it may well be that even works avowedly committed to laying bare the social roots of culture manage, in practice, to lapse into culturalism. Such is, in my view, the case of Mannheim's 'sociology of culture'—perhaps the first influential presentation of this branch of social science. Mannheim proposed the sociology of culture as a natural extension of his famous brainchild, the 'sociology of knowledge'. In contrast with the latter, his sociological study of culture aimed at covering the entire range of social symbolism: not only discursive thinking but art and religion as well; but the new formula was also intended to render the awesome German 'Geist'—too meaningful a term to be simply translated by 'spirit'.[11] Moreover, as an analytic perspective, it was chiefly directed as replacing the depiction of ideologies *as by-products and reflexes* of social situations, prevalent in books like *Ideology and Utopia* and in his brilliant monograph on conservative thought,[12] by a less deterministic and holistic handling of ideational dynamics.[13]

The trouble is that the will to escape holistic a-priori-isms, even at the cost of advocating a tactic sociological nominalism, seems to have been conflated in Mannheim with the old, perverted mental habit of German Geisteswissenschaften: their ingrained cultural-ism, fostered by their distinctively idealistic origins. So Mannheim, the man who fought German idealism in the name of the social conditioning of ideas, came to loosen the ties between thought and society to the point of nearly obliterating the causal meaning of their relationship. His worst idealistic claims concerning the mythical free-floating of modern planning intellectuals were already prefigured by the slippery vagueness of social determin-ations in his essay on the intelligentsia.[14] The 'sociology of culture' was a born culturalism.

Unlike Mannheim's, the most illuminating amidst recent contributions to the sociological theory of culture have no place for idealistic equivocations. In Geertz's semiotic culturology, for instance, culture 'is not a *power*, something to which social events, behaviours, institutions, or processes can be causally attributed; it is a *context*, something within which they can be intelligibly . . . described'.[15]

However, *what about the causal study of the context itself?* Granted that culture can be illuminatingly seen as a framework lending intelligibility to events, behaviours and institutions; but what should one do when it comes to explaining that very framework? The truth is that just as it is no use taking culture for a 'power' giving birth to societal processes, so to think of such processes as a power directly originating culture will not do either. One can never simply deduce cultural effects from the state of 'material' infrastructures, for the material infrastructures them-selves, in their set up as well as in their operation, actually depend on a cultural frame. No human practice could possibly be without the structuring assistance of culture, its codes and patterns. So, if culture context is not a 'power', neither is that to which it serves as a context. 'Culture' is not an epiphenomenon of 'society': otherwise, why should it exist at all? Culture is decidedly too big a thing—too embracing a dimension of the social being—to be just a redundancy, a lusus historiae as it were.

Culturalism, as we have seen, is question-begging: it is unconvincing because it tries to explain culture by itself. Sociologism, on the other hand, ends not by explaining culture but (since it treats it as an epiphenomenon) by explaining it away. Fortunately, the anticulturalist caveat needs not take the form of sociologism: it may consist just in a certain *sense of infrastructure*.

Still, there are at least two ways of practicing an infrastructuralist approach to culture and, in particular, to culture change. One of them consists in taking sides in the venerable debate about the causal primacy of either super- or infrastructure. Let us just pick up some instances among those widely quoted in the literature. A good one is Steward's hierarchy of 'core institutions'[16] whereby society adapts to and exploits the environment: techno-economics conditions sociopolitical organization, and this in turn the ideological level; change may start anywhere in society, even outside the core institutions—but unless it affects the latter in their stratigraphic structure, society as a whole will not be substantially altered (the agon of ideology-induced change and infrastructural resistance in underdeveloped countries provides a vivid illustration). Another, narrower example of infrastructural determination can be found in Nimkoff and Middleton's comparative enquiry into types of family and forms of economy. They concluded that family types changed according to the technoeconomic basis[17]: the conjugal family prevails in hunting-and-gathering and industrial economies; the extended family, in horticultural or agricultural societies (the extent of demand for social labour provides the societal intervening variable).

In view of several similar statements of infrastructural causation, Marvin Harris claimed that the 'cultural-materialist strategy' has proven itself remarkably more productive than its opponents, on which the onus of sociological proof should accordingly be henceforth incumbent.[18] Nevertheless, the infrastructuralist tenet requires serious qualification. By and large, the assessment of the relative causal tenor of social sub-systems remains an open, empirical question.[19] As Gouldner and Peterson surmised in their quantitative survey of the determining and predictive value of technology, social structure and the 'moral order', the first—the most infrastructural of the factors under examination—seems to be more decisive than the other two—but then, the moral sphere appears to count *more* than social structure.[20] Similarly, Yehudi Cohen found that while technology prevails over the polity in change within stateless society, in nation-states the political level tends to command technological transformations (the polity is as often as not incorporated into the superstructure, ever since Marx').[21]

The lesson to be drawn is clear enough. Infrastructuralism should be posited as a *methodological* device rather than as a substantive assertion. We cannot prejudge the importance of infrastructural factors, nor can we ascertain in any generic, a priori way the fact, or the degree, of their control over superstructures and ideological formations, any more than we can assess the predominance of the latter over the former. Such is, in effect, as we briefly saw, the conclusion invariably reached by practically all outstanding studies aimed at assessing the respective weight of infra- or superstructural elements, and, in particular, by the last of the series, Eric Carlton's *Ideology and Social Order*—a careful comparison between Old Kingdom Egypt and ancient Athens, devoted to probing the causal strength of mechanisms of social control grounded on ideological patterns. There is definitely no ready-made map of infrastructure at the disposal of social scientists in their endeavours to explain either culture or social structure.

Why should, then, the social scientist be at all a (methodological) infrastructuralist? The reason for being one lies, I suppose, in the very discipline of scientific cognition—sociological or not. *Scientific* knowledge, unlike the cognitive ambitions of the religious experience, is committed to 'the machine ideal of explanation'.[22] Mechanism, in turn, may be seen as an epistemological affection for economical explanatory models, that is models whose properties as a whole derive as strictly as possible from the properties of its parts and their arrangements, these primary properties being few, well defined and intelligible.[23] This *elementarism of mechanism* presides, indeed, over our image of scientific explanation.

Explanation, in effect, ultimately amounts to passing from a 'colourful' level of reality to another less colourful, *but more structured*, one. Explaining goes always from multifarious secondary qualities to a limited number of underlying mechanisms. In this sense, all explanation is a *reduction*: remember Newton's mechanics, resolutely ignoring a host of sensory data in order to explain physical motion; or again, Marx's way of looking at his own attempt to lay bare the mechanics of capitalism.

Reduction is not an altogether popular word among social scientists. In the 'human' sciences, we very often think of an intellectually *unsatisfactory* explanation as precisely a reduction. Whenever a sociological explanation seems to impoverish the explanandum, or seems too inclined to treat it as a mere epiphenomenon, we readily speak of 'reductionism'; and many a humanist social scientist ends by thinking of reductionism as the epitome of reduction. Nevertheless, every true explanatory reduction actually implies from the start *the recognition of levels of reality*. Otherwise, how could anything be reduced to anything else? By the same token, 'reductionisms'—misfired explanations that explain their explananda away by degrading them to the condition of gratuitous epiphenomena—could not be farther from the true spirit of reduction; for the essence of reductionism is its obstinacy in ignoring that reality is composed of *several* levels, all ontologically legitimate (though, admittedly, varying in the degree of their ontological density). In the last analysis, reductionism is actually a misnomer: while the word suggests a reinforcement of reduction, the thing denotes rather an *avoidance* of reduction. Reduction feeds on the epistemic tension between different levels of reality, whereas reductionism thrives on a false homogenization of reality, with no room left for any veritable epistemological tension.

After all, if, as Nagel (*The Structure of Science*, ch. 11) shows, (1) reduction always operates through the *deduction* of a set of statements (e.g. about temperature) from other sets of statements (e.g. about molecular energy), and if (2) such a deduction always involves the use of *connecting* statements of some kind, *the latter are by no means statements of synonymity*. In old-fashioned scientific terminology: effects and causes are never synonymous. *Theories*, not concepts, are what is reduced: concepts describing 'temperature' are not in the least victimized by their being explained by concepts denoting 'molecular energy'.

The humanist conflation of reduction and reductionism often springs from an alleged concern with preserving a sense of complexity in science. The humanists fear that reduction means over-simplification. However, scientific explanation consists not so much in simplifying as in substituting 'a more intelligible complexity for a less intelligible one'.[24] Modern philosophy of science finds no difficulty in acknowledging 'irreducible variety' and 'logical contingency' as fundamental features of the cosmos; bearing them firmly in mind, modern naturalism insists on defining itself as a *contextualistic* naturalism.[25] There is of course no contradiction between positing an irreducible complexity as a trait *of the world* and the inherence of reduction *in the mind's* cognitive behaviour.

Significantly, awareness of contextual complexity is to be found nowadays precisely amidst social theorists who, while being inimical to the neo-idealist epistemology of either pheno-menologists or Wittgensteinians, do cling to the 'machine ideal of explanation'. Gellner, for instance, for whom epistemological materialism is but another name for mechanism, or structuralism (since what counts in the materialist approach to explanation is not the sense of matter as stuff but rather the sense of structure), is also the first to propose, as a general method in social science, a 'multiform materialism' which would unite *alertness to contexts* to that indispensable *search for determinisms* inherent in all genuine explanatory enterprise.[26]

However, the most important thing about reduction qua scientific explanation remains to be said. It is that reductive knowledge, i.e. true scientific cognition, always operates *against identity*.[27] Science progresses through destroying the self-images of mankind. The pattern is well-known: every major revolution in science entailed a ruthless dismissal of anthropocentric illusions. So with Copernicus, so with Darwin—and so, at least in principle, with Freud. As Piaget has it, science always advances through *decentring* steps in so far as our collective ego is concerned.[28]

Now, as Aron suggests, the 'infrastructure theme' in sociology boils down to something essentially akin to such de-anthropocentring strategy. What, in fact, infrastructuralism commits the sociologist to is a refusal 'to take men at their word'.[29] The gist of the matter is a refusal to accept as a final truth what men say or think they are and they do. In as much as every real social scientist is bound to work this way, the infrastructure theme is indeed the central perspective in the sociological mind: the perspective which embodies the bold spirit of cognitive reduction in social science.

Infrastructuralism, then, amounts to no more than an epistemo-logical path, or a cognitive strategy. It is the path that Marx and Engels once termed an ascent 'from earth to heaven'.[30] From earth to heaven, since it starts with men in the flesh, taken in their actual life-processes, instead of taking for granted 'men as narrated', i.e. mankind as self-imagined. The great advantage of so doing lies in the recovery of what idealism—the from-heaven-to-earth path—conspicuously lacks: a *sense of constraints*, the equivalent, in society, of those underlying mechanisms in which physical science locates the primary elements of natural phenomena. For, if man is indeed the author of his own history, history as a rule seldom corresponds to his intentions; social science is by and large the study of the unintended consequences of human groups' action—consequences, that is, largely moulded by the constraints the environment and the other groups impose on every collective, let alone individual, endeavour.

Infrastructuralism, as Aron rightly adds, is never, *in principle* a dogmatic stance. It only becomes one when sociologists engage in scholastic debates over reifying images of the infrastructure, relentlessly and barrenly asking what determines what, *in genere* and per omnia saecula. Basically, however, the only commandment of the infrastructure theme is to seek the true causes of men's actions amidst the humdrum universe of the constraints of practical reality. Infrastructure, in this sense, is less a set of things than of relations. Ultimately, *it is a way of seeing through, not any self-evident substratum of the social being*. Aron's caveat strikingly reinforces our previous distinction to the effect of treating infrastructure as an epistemological path (implying a methodological behaviour), rather than as an ontological subject.

'Infrastructure' is a conspicuously topological metaphor. Nevertheless, one should take care not to give it the wrong spatial meaning; for what it denotes, at least in right if seldom in practice, is not a 'region' of reality—it is rather a *dimension* of it. The best way to avoid the shortcomings attending the reifying notions of infrastructure is to keep in mind its 'perceptual' connotations. Infrastructuralism should primarily be conceived of as an optical device, rather than as any objective causal process—something like perspective in classical painting: a property of reality, but even more a method for organizing perceptual data, a way of relating the observed to the observer; for, as Jakubowski remarked forty years ago, nothing could be more misleading than to think of the differentiation between base and superstructure as an absolute objective distinction between two different, un-overlapping spheres.[31]

The mistake of seeing infra- and superstructure as un-overlapping comes straight from an objectivist, reifying cast of mind. It may take the form of a crude separation between (social) being and consciousness—a particularly misguided idea, since on the one hand, consciousness permeates social being throughout life, even at the most 'material' levels of the latter, while, on the other hand, superstructure does not consist only of ideas in abstracto but is often regarded as comprehending 'material' aspects such as political relations and therefore cannot be identified with any disembodied 'consciousness'.[32]

The objectivist illusion may also take the more usual form of a stratigraphic scheme slicing up social reality into layers. The layers can embrace the infrastructure-superstructure whole (as we saw in Steward's case) or they can be slices of just one of these two fundamental levels, as in the once prestigious three-storyed division by Brinkmann of the content of the superstructure into law and custom, science and technology, art and religion.[33] One can even distinguish lower and higher spheres within each infra- or superstructural layer. Scheler, for instance, divided religion into four levels: popular piety; ritual customs and cult; the charismatic visions of homines religiosi; and, finally, the metaphysical ideas about the deity and the salvation, the last two being considerably freer from the grip of Realfaktoren than the first two.[34]

Because they retain the suggestive power of the original metaphor of verticality which infrastructuralism feeds on, these ingenious architectures are all the more attractive. Unfortunately, nearly every close look at them reveals hopeless difficulties. We have already seen how the causal order of Steward's 'core institutions' varies, according to major differences in historical context (pp. 66–7). As for Brinkmann's three-storeyed Überbau, it omits altogether a central issue for modern sociology: the problem of the social function of science. From Marx's time to the present day, science has increasingly been acknowledged as a productive force. The so-called second industrial revolution is first and foremost the result of a 'science takes command' drive in industrial production. Consequently, a conception which places science as an un-overlapping sphere of the superstructure is of little avail for the analysis of contemporary society.

Scores of similar theoretical impasses forced both Marxism and the sociology of knowledge (the main trustees of the infrastructure idea), since their very beginnings, to devise flexibilizing conceptual bridges destined to cope with the gaps in their infrastructural explanations. The 'dialectical' interplay of infra- and super-structural factors has been relentlessly emphasized; 'ultimate' determination by the basis has been clumsily combined with the acknowledgment of the 'partial autonomy' of superstructural spheres like the polity or 'ideological formations' in the sense of belief systems. However, as Merton rightly observed, the more the theory of infrastructural determination becomes cluttered with such an array of 'dialectical' master-keys, the less it retains a fulcrum of testable, falsifiable hypotheses.[35] Overflexibilized, the theory comes to explain too much; deprived of specifying statements susceptible to being invalidated by counter-evidences, it loses in explanatory power all that it had tried to gain in sophistication and comprehensiveness.

The nemesis of reifying objectivism dooms infrastructuralism to explanatory impotence. Marxist anthropology often used to bear witness to this. Post-Lévi-Straussian *marxisant* anthropology has by now shed a considerable amount of Marxist clichés. For example, Maurice Godelier (*Horizon, trajets marxistes en anthropologie*) has argued that in several primitive societies kinship systems do not derive from relations of production but rather *function* as such. He also holds that the relation between infra- and superstructure should be interpreted as referring to a hierarchy of *functions*, not of institutional levels; but in the 1950s, this kind of sophistication was not at all the rule among *marxisant* anthropologists. Thus, when Peter Worsley attacked Oxford structuralism by claiming that kinship systems are, no matter their unifying function in tribal culture, themselves but the expression of economic activities, Meyer Fortes was at no pains in replying that one cannot impute the structure of the Tallensi lineage systems to economic relations as an effect to a cause.[36] In other words, the adoption of an unabashed objectivist infrastructural approach entailed the conversion of the materialist perspective into a crude economism, ironically at odds with even the way the Marxist vulgate depicts 'primitive' social formations.

Understandably, this kind of misfired explanation nourishes the scepticism of some anthropologists—not particularly ill-disposed towards Marxist social theory—as regards the idea of infra-structure as a whole. Thus Sahlins, commenting on the Worsley-Fortes controversy, sees the absence of differentiation between the social sub-systems in primitive culture as a lack of differentiation 'between base and superstructure'.[37] Yet the two are quite distinct things. That economy, polity and religion do not appear as separate 'systems' in tribal society does not in the least mean that base and superstructure cannot be discerned in it—provided that we cease to envisage the latter, in reifying fashion, as *regions* of the social fabric and regard them as *dimensional aspects*. (It is a pity that Sahlins, too influenced by Habermas's culturalism and Baudrillard's wildly speculative semiotic approach to social theory, did not pause to consider the explanatory chances of such a sound *methodological* infrastructuralism.)

Indeed, as anyone barely familiar with anthropological literature knows, for every 'bad' infrastructuralist explanation like Worsley's, there is at least one major attempt at a sound one. The literature is full of cogent hypotheses which explain a given superstructure in terms of infrastructure without explaining away the former, or unilaterally presenting the latter as an ontologically objective stratum of social reality. A good example is provided by Gluckman's well-known analysis of the link between (magic) beliefs and the structure of social relations in African tribal society.[38]

African tribes, says Gluckman, were stationary economies with rudimentary technology, where man possessed only simple tools and produced little more than what he himself consumed. Standards of living were therefore as egalitarian as meagre. There were 'rich' men who got power from their wealth, but they were practically unable to employ the latter to reach higher standards of living. Above all, they could not use wealth to exploit labour (for instance, there was no undertaking in which masters could invest the surplus products of slave work); the narrow scope of exploitation allowed by the production system precluded the emergence of social classes. Now, in these tribes, any man who was unusually enterprising or too much lucky tended to suspect he was in danger of being bewitched, and to be suspected by others of resorting to witchcraft to 'steal' their riches and their luck. As most social relations not only embraced many interests at the same time but were also face to face, unintegrated in any large impersonal institutional frame work, all events came to be attributed to some cause springing from these *personal* relations. So every misfortune was felt as a tort, the work of a witch. In the political sphere, blames were also cast according to this personalistic pattern. Acts of injustice were always seen as individual, not social. Kings were often blamed; kingship, never.

Here, in witchcraft and in rebellion alike, ideological super-structures such as magic belief or political protest remain strongly moulded by an infrastructure represented by the overwhelming predominance of a 'primary group' type of social interaction. Unequivocally committed to explaining social creeds and attitudes by a social 'basis', Gluckman does not indulge in any culturalistic question-begging; yet, unlike Worsley, he avoids as consistently the fallacy of hypostatizing social bases by resorting to an 'objectivist', a-priori-istic model stating a rigid 'primacy of the infrastructure'—the kind of pseudo-materialistic thinking which once made MacRae (in *Ideology and Society*) label Marxism as 'the lazy man's sociology'. Instead, Gluckman evinces both a sense of social determinism and a sense of social context. His way of elucidating a certain 'culture' with the help of its social structure—a non-'reductionist' reduction —is in fact a nice piece of what we mean by *methodological* infrastructuralism.

Besides, (methodological) infrastructuralism alone can correct (objectivist) infrastructuralism. The only way to improve explana-tions by infrastructure is to find subtler infrastructuralist approaches, not to return to deceptive ideas about allegedly self-supporting superstructures. Consider, for instance, the evo-lution of historiography in the case of the French Revolution. Nearly all its first influential historians proved themselves to be downright idealists when it came to ascertaining the causes of those portentous events. The romantic liberalism of Michelet saw the fall of the Bastille as a triumph of 'le peuple' over Catholicism—but for Michelet, 'the people' was just the bearer of a living principle', Justice; similarly, its arch-enemy, the Church, meant only a 'doctrine'—the dessicated dogma of Grace. Later in the century, the fanatic anti-romantic, Taine, identifying the Revolution with the Terror, found the main origin of Jacobin terrorism in the exacerbation of the 'raison raisonnante'—that fatal abstract rationalism of the French classical mind, inherited and intensified by the philosophes. Thus, in Michelet's democratic commendation and in Taine's reactionary condemnation alike, the basic causes of the Great Revolution were thought to be *ideas*; both historians quite overlooked the influence of social or economic infra-structures.

Not surprisingly, twentieth-century revolutionary historiography began in reaction against such a patent disregard for Realfaktoren. From 1900 (with Jaurès) through the 1920s (with Mathiez) up to the

1940s (with Lefebvre) the Revolution was chiefly attributed, in the then standard Marxist fashion, to the rise of a capitalistic bourgeoisie bound to overthrow an anachronic 'feudal' social order. Meanwhile, however, the results of the work of two generations of economic historians (Sée, Labrousse, Lefebvre himself, etc.) showed beyond the shadow of a doubt that, on the one hand, the revolutionary bourgeoisie was overwhelmingly bureaucratic, rather than entrepreneurial, while, on the other hand, by 1789 feudalism, even in the Marxist sense of a specific form of labour exploitation, was either absent from French agriculture or just playing the role of a vestigial framework of domination employed with thoroughly capitalistic aims. In the French eighteenth-century countryside, feudalism and capitalism were not actually antagonistic: in the words of Le Roy Ladurie, they were rather 'accomplices'. No wonder the feudalism-to-capitalism view of the decade opened in French history at that annus mirabilis came to be denounced by the late Alfred Cobban as a 'myth'.[39]

Yet, as the same historian is the first to stress, to discard this 'myth of the French Revolution' is not, of course, to suggest that the Revolution itself was mythical. The removal of privileges paved the way for a 'career-open-to-talent' society;[40] the dropping of the payment of residual seigneurial dues achieved the emancipation of the peasantry; several of the legal reforms enacted by the revolutionary assemblies were as liberating as far-reaching. The French Revolution was indeed a vast (if not, in every aspect, a deep) *social* transformation—even though its very success, notably by strengthening small-scale property, *delayed* rather than fostered the modernization of French capitalism. Tocqueville had detected an important continuity between the Revolution and the Ancien Régime with respect of political centralization; Albert Sorel had no less persuasively interpreted its foreign politics as carrying on the plurisecular work of the monarchy. To a certain point, historians tend nowadays to see the social results of the Revolution as the epitome of regressive trends. From a 'developmentalist' viewpoint based on the growth of big enterprise, the Revolution was actually a serious setback. François Crouzet went as far as speaking of an (economic) 'national catastrophe'.

A hasty mind would jump to the conclusion that the critical demolition of the feudalism-to-capitalism explanation marks a striking defeat of infrastructuralism. Is not the rise-of-the-capitalistic-bourgeoisie thesis couched in the Marxist idiom, the native language of infrastructuralist views about social causation? Certainly it is; but, from the rejection of a (by and large) *false* social basis as cause of the Revolution, it does not follow that a more plausible cause is not to be sought in other, presumably truer, social bases. Indeed, as we examine the kind of factors whereby contemporary historiography replaced the largely mythical entities, feudal order and capitalistic bougeoisie, we find that they are at least as 'infrastructural' as their unwarranted predecessors. The bourgeois-but-non-capitalist lawyers and officials who lead the Revolution and the no longer feudal aristocrats who were crushed by it are social classes, not anything even remotely similar, in the ontology of society, to the disembodied ideas to which Taine or Michelet attached prime importance in the making of history.

While objectivist infrastructuralism—in its most usual guise, a dogmatic assertion of the primacy of the economic—turned out to be not a bit less fanciful than its culturalist alternatives, the best empirical research on the causes of the Revolution in no way relinquished the sense of infrastructure. In historical as well as in sociological explanation, what an ill-conceived infrastructuralism has mythicized, only methodological infrastructuralism can demystify. Now, methodological infrastructuralism, as we have just seen, is not less of an 'infra' determination—in fact, it is *more* of it. It is the objectivist, the *hypostatizing* approach to infrastructure, not the strictly methodological one, that enslaved the explanation of the French Revolution to a philosophical history only apparently less idealist than its spiritualist counterparts. Superficially, the abandonment of sweeping economist theses in pointing out the causes of the Revolution seems a 'retreat from materialism'; at a closer look, it proves infinitely more empirically minded than the speculative reconstructions of a-priori-istic infrastructuralism, and therefore, much more faithful to a genuine, scientific 'materialism'. In short, rickety infrastructural explanations are to be replaced by sounder ones, not by explanations of the opposite kind; the cure of degenerate infrastructuralism is always a homoeopathy.

To be sure, the anti-a-priori-istic, non-hypostatizing approach to infrastructural determination can sometimes be no more than the jargon of a certain philosophical sociology, only too eager to rescue idealistically the picture of society from the bonds of social determinisms for the sake of elusive 'totalities' asserted in wilfully speculative fashion, as in Lukács's *History and Class Conscious-*

ness and its numerous descent; but if we take care to avoid metaphysical acrobatics, methodological infrastructuralism can be, as several historical analyses show, a powerful empirical-minded strategy, full of explanatory suggestiveness. Indicative rather than elaborate though they are, such analyses will endeavour to conform to the aforesaid epistemological spirit.

In particular—last but not least—there seems to be no other way of, explaining *cultural changes*. In fact, as Geertz perceptively stressed, as long as sociological theory treats culture and society as 'mirror images' of each other—as long as it does not fully, if only analytically, dissociate a cultural superstructure from a societal basis, and learn to grasp the frequently crucial *discontinuities* between the two, there can only be little hope as to the ability of social science to explain change; for change very often springs, as in Geertz's Javanese examples, from gaps between the cultural framework of meaning and the patterns of social interaction.[41] Exactly the same reasoning applies to the study of social symbolics in their transformations. As a highly sympathetic critic of psychoanalysis remarked, because Freud paid little attention to social structure, it is unclear in his thought how one symbolic succeeds another;[42] which means that, for all its invaluable sense of the symbolism of the repressed, psychoanalysis—an indispensable auxiliary to the sociology of culture—requires to be supported by a methodological infrastructuralism.

Geertz's wise vindication of the analytical separateness of culture and social structure is not couched in the language of infrastructure (hence its easy utilization by a sophisticated and very much change-concerned functionalist like Sztompka, who finds no difficulty in translating Geertz's phrasing in the theory of social sub-systems). In subscribing to this non-isomorphic view of the culture/social structure relationship, we seem to return to our preliminary considerations on the twin vices of culturalism and sociologism, rather than to elaborate the theory of infrastructure proper; but this is only apparently so: for in the sociology of culture, the infrastructure theme may be considered a kind of radicalization of the anticulturalist position. Indeed, in the sociology of culture, infrastructuralism should begin by discerning 'culture' from 'society' in order to forestall any collapse into culturalisms (of which normative determinism is only the most conspicuous variety); but having begun this way, it is further supposed to attempt a reduction of the societal basis taken to be the determining factors of cultural explananda. Epistemologically, then, methodological infrastructuralism is anticulturalism with a vengeance.

A cogent application of a robust infrastructuralist approach to cultural change in which the societal basis is related to still 'harder' variables has just been put forward by the French historian, Pierre Chaunu, in his research on the origins of the Reformation. Let us end the present considerations by summarizing his fascinating conclusions.

The Reformation notoriously sprang from a crisis in cultural legitimacy—a breakdown of legitimacy in religious authority. Now according to Chaunu and his research team,[43] from the middle of the thirteenth century, Western Christendom, after a long populational rise, entered a very long period characterized by the passage from an essentially 'frontier' society to the closed world of demographic density. This wide and lasting transformation reinforced the economic role of the nuclear family. The 'frontier' being closed, new conditions of tilling and land-owning emerged, which pushed the nuclear family to free itself from the grips of the larger descent groups. The primacy of the nuclear family entailed in turn a setback in the marrying age. The spread of celibacy bred a sexual asceticism in the masses, and the new libidinal pattern generated the emotional grounds for the craving for lay religion, for direct, personal mystical and soteriological experiences, so characteristic throughout the pre-Reformation period. The traditional mediaeval separation between an élite of religious virtuosi (the regular clergy) and a passive mass laity[44] could no longer retain its time-honoured legitimacy. Increasingly, the Church began to lose or share its spiritual monopoly. With the devotio moderna, the imitatio Christi became more and more democratic. Meanwhile, humanism taught the intelligentsia to refuse any blind acceptance of tradition, and the 'coming of the book[45] disseminated literacy at an unprecedented pace in pre-industrial society. Seen from this perspective, Luther was less a beginning than a (however catalytic) culmination. After all, the gist of the matter had already been aptly expressed by the Catholic Erasmus: 'monachatus non est pietas'. . . but Luther played, of course, a crucial, decisive role: as the first modern reformer, he provided the legitimation long awaited for by the outbursts of popular religiosity. His was a breakthrough in legitimacy-making.

I deliberately omitted from the picture the influence of

politico-ecclesiastic events (including the most momentous ones, such as the quarrel between the Holy See and the Empire, or the Great Schism) in order to underline the interplay of more impersonal 'longue durée' factors. Chaunu's variables, the demographic evolution, the new land economy, the new status of the nuclear family, sexual deprivation, the long wave of lay mysticism and the new literacy level, constitute a pretty set of factors, coming from distinct areas of social reality and engaged in a complex pattern of mutually supporting co-variations. So much for the 'sense of context'. On the other hand, these variables seem to be sufficiently 'hierarchized' to present also a similar sense of determinism.

Admittedly, were we to claim for such a picture of the prehistory of the Reformation the status of a strict explanatory theory, based on all the rules of valid inference, the looseness of its logical structure would at once come up. In several points, these co-variations could be easily counter-exemplified. Though their interrelatedness is quite convincing, its logical necessity in terms of a deductive-nomological explanation is far from established: in particular, some of the 'responses' to the infrastructural stimuli reckoned by Chaunu were not in this sense the only possible ones; they seem to allow of what Hempel calls 'explanatory over-determination',[46] thus casting serious doubts upon the explana-toriness of the 'theory'. Arguing that 'this is how it happened, anyway', will not do, since we are not questioning the factual occurrence of any of these variables, nor, indeed, of them all; we are just wanting to measure the causal weight of their vicinity in a given period of Western history.

Yet none of these strictures detracts from the soundness of the approach. Some of Chaunu's premises may have to be checked or improved but nobody would deny the explanatory suggestiveness with which he brought to the fore a number of factors that powerfully add to our realization of the causes of the Reformation. Social historians like Chaunu are born methodological infra-structuralists—and if history is by far the most solid and developed among the social sciences, this is largely due to an intuitive fidelity to the 'theme of infrastructure'.

(1977)

4   Psychology in its place (a note)

'Methodological individualism' is the pivot of what has been perhaps the fiercest theoretical debate in Anglo-Saxon, and especially British, sociology in the 1950s and 1960s. As is well known, methodological individualism is the claim that all explanations of social phenomena are *ultimately* to be phrased as statements about individual behaviour, not as statements about alleged social 'wholes'.

Since Hayek's now historical first shot, aimed at separating the concepts which guide individual actions from people's theorizing about their own behaviour,[1] this claim led a rich and troubled life. The main stages and viewpoints have recently been concisely anthologized by Jarvie.[2] For all practical purposes, reference may be here restricted to three interventions:

(a) first, Agassi's[3] refinement of the argument through his
distinction between *ontological* and *methodological*
individualism. The former denies the *existence* of social wholes;
the latter disclaims *only that they can have aims*;
(b) second, Gellner's contention that our individual dispositions
are neither factually nor logically independent of the social
context where they arise—as well as, in a more picturesque vein,
his warning: that history is 'about chaps' does not in the least
entail constructing explanations of historical processes 'in terms
of chaps';[4]
(c) third, Steven Lukes's excellent general critique. Lukes
promptly dispels false assumptions often associated with

sociological individualistic epistemology, such as the idea that
social phenomena are: (1) less easily observable than individual
ones (If so, what about a person's intentions, surely less easy to
grasp than some social processes, like the procedure of a court?);
or (2) harder to understand (but again, compare the court's
procedure with the obscure motives of a criminal); or (3)
anyhow, existentially dependent on individuals (true, 'army' is
just a plural of 'soldier'; but then, it is no less true that we can
only speak of soldiers in so far as we can speak of armies).

Having rejected such false assumptions, Lukes distinguishes two
general classes of *individual predicates*:

(1) those which, like brain-states or 'instincts' (e.g., aggression),
while presupposing or not consciousness, do *not* basically
presuppose any social context; and
(2) those which, whether general behaviour like power and
co-operation, or then more specific conducts (e.g., cashing
cheques, or voting) *do* presuppose a social context.

Among individual predicates of class (2), those of the second
type alone (cashing cheques, voting) not only presuppose a social
context but essentially *refer, in their constitutive meaning, to
specific features of groups or institutions*. Now, in every attempt to
explain this kind of phenomenon, these relevant specific aspects of
the social context are necessarily incorporated into the description
of that very individual (voter, etc.) to whom methodological
individualism commands us to turn in order to account for the
social process. In other words, such individualistic explanations are
always question-begging, since they invariably build their explanandum—the social—into the purportedly individual explanans.[5]
Therefore, it seems, one can safely practise a methodological
infrastructuralism in the study of matters cultural without being
haunted by the methodological *individualism* bogey: quod erat
demonstrandum. No wonder many exercises in historical sociology,
like Weber's nationalization thesis or Gellner's sociology of
Transition (to industrialism and modernity), evince a strong sense
of social interaction without subscribing to analysis 'in terms of
chaps'. Only *ultimately* are they translatable into statements about
(myriads of) individual acts—and then, rather trivially.
Besides, even social interaction itself (apart from dogmatic
methodological individualism) is—pace ethnomethodology—a

poor explanans. As Percy Cohen pointed out, action theory is at most 'a set of near-tautological assumptions which structure the mode of cognition of social inquiry, which is, on the whole, concerned with the conditions and the products of social interaction'.[6] It is not enough, as Piaget[7] believes, to go from ideology to *behavioural* infrastructure: one must get at the conditions of behaviour, which are never thoroughly interactional. Praxis is always mediated by what (be it, to a large measure, from human origin) not only does not act but refuses to be acted upon.

Does this recognition leave methodological infrastructuralism fundamentally out of touch with the *psychological* dimension of social existence? The role of psychology in sociological explanation is an affair still vaster than the issues raised by the holism/individualism debate. Yet here again, I think, we can harmlessly confine ourselves to a handful of sobering remarks. To begin with, let us not forget that not all methodological individualisms are psychologistic in the sense of subjectivistic: as is widely known, Popper's, for one, is not, and explicitly purports to replace Mill's psychological sociology by an *objectivist* assessment of the 'logic of the situation' (which agrees with the Popperian regard for institutional analysis[8]). Could it be, then, that psychologism is on the part of holism? In order to avoid semantic entanglements, it is wise to consider the following reasons, which are mutually qualifying but not contradictory.

Those who postulate a determining role of psychological factors in social life often fail to distinguish the mind (or personality, etc.) as a biological phenomenon from the mind as culturally shaped. The former does not seem to qualify as a primum movens of cultural evolution because since a very distant past man has remained anatomically and physiologically basically the same, while culture and society have undergone deep and frequent changes. On the other hand, the mind qua culturally shaped is certainly an agency of social determination, but logically this just amounts to no more than saying that culture determines itself.[9] The so-called culture-and-personality school is a good example: it tried to build socialization (in the form of child-rearing patterns) into an independent variable; nevertheless, the available empirical evidence indicates that socialization techniques followed institutional changes, not the other way round.[10]

True, sociologism, typified by Durkheim, fails to acknowledge that every allegedly sociological purism willy-nilly relies, in the last analysis, on psychological assumptions. Inkeles rightly observed how Durkheim himself presupposed a human 'psychic constitution' as the root of the need for self-transcending.[11] Runciman[12] goes as far as to claim the need for 'standing Comte on his head': according to him, the science which stands to human history as pure to applied is psychology. (Incidentally, the same view was held by Freud, who once wrote that there are only two sciences, psychology and natural science,[13] sociology amounting to no more than 'applied psychology'.) Sociology, like history and anthropology (from both of which it differs only in technique), is a law-consuming, not a law-producing, discipline; now, its main theoretical grounding cannot but be composed of borrowings from psychology. Runciman is a methodological individualist, though he hastens to add that this does not amount to requiring that the terms of any statement about institution be 'translated . . . into extensionally equivalent psychological terms'.[14] We find here an unexpected reversal of Popper's tandem, methodological individualism cum antipsychologism.

Even if we grant just the constant occurrence of psychological assumptions, not Runciman's ambitious grounding role for psychology, it does not in the least follow that psychological factors enjoy any privileged *causal* status. In point of fact social psychologists like Barbu are the first to warn that 'motivation analysis can seldom, if ever, take the place of causal analysis'.[15] As the historian, Peter Gay, recently put it: all history is in some measure psycho-history, yet psycho-history cannot be *all* of history.[16]

Is it necessary to stress that the point here is not at all inimical to the sociological use of psychological factors? Coming as they do from social scientists deeply interested in psychology (and, of course, depth psychology), these warnings do not in the least disavow the crucial importance of psychological elements *as intervening variables*. Inkeles's showcase carries conviction: in their sociological study on suicide, Henry and Short followed Durkheim in taking the experience of social integration for the independent variable, and the varying rates of suicide for the dependent one; but they introduced a psychological novelty— childhood systems of punishment, either physical or moral—which played the role of an intervening mechanism. Ekeh sees in McClelland's social psychology, focused on the 'achieving personality', the basis for an analogous rephrasing of Weber's

Protestant ethic thesis: Calvinism would be the independent variable; the 'spirit of capitalism', the dependent one; and the process of socializing into independence in Protestant upbringing, which leads to high rates of 'achievement motivation', would feature as the psychological intervening variables.[17]

(1977)

5 The symbolic; or culture, value and symbol

The stabilization of the culture concept in modern anthropological practice accredited a distinction between culture, understood as a set of values and ideas, and social interaction. We have seen (p. 50) how the difference between British and American usages tended in part to overlap such a dichotomy. However, in the long run, on a theoretical level the dualism of value pattern and role network was given full citizenship in social science: the former became the subject-matter of the theory of culture; the second, of the theory of social structure. In their influential 1958 joint paper on 'The concepts of culture and social system', Kroeber and Parsons sponsored this conceptual convention, contrasting culture, 'transmitted and created patterns of values, ideas, and other meaningful systems of factors in the shaping of human behaviour' with 'the relational system of interactions among individuals and collectivities'.[1] In brief: the cultural and the societal.

On the other hand, nearly all of the authors that so conceive of culture stress its *symbolic* dimension. Here again, Kroeber's underwriting of the identification of culture with 'ways of thinking, feeling and reacting acquired and transmitted *by symbols*' set the tone.

Now we must dwell for a while on both these aspects: first, on the general symbolic nature of culture processes; second, on the idea that values are the core of culture.

At first sight, the symbolic aspect is easier to handle. Considered in its utmost generality, the fact that culture uses symbols boils down simply to underlining man's ability to attach *meaning* to experience—meaning that, as a rule, overflows the hic et nunc of the experienced. Anthropologists often emphasized the active role played by man—as distinct from animal—in freely assigning values to vocal stimuli; White made the symbolic competence into one of his major evolutionary contributions to superorganicism.[2] Today, taking into account the remarkable findings in animal psychology and ethology which rendered us familiar with the idea of infra-human symbolic communication, as well as the views of structural linguistics, they prefer to think that what tells man from animal is not so much the simple 'skill of introducing symbolic go-betweens into the space which divides awareness of the event from the event itself',[3] but, rather, the faculty of endlessly reproducing and producing new symbolic structures.

Such capacity is based on that uniquely human phenomenon called by Martinet[4] the 'double articulation' (morphemic and phonemic) of language. The human talent for assuming 'explanatory attitudes' towards sign-stimuli, instead of simply displaying stereotyped reactions to them, man's competence to enact 'reflective choices', delaying responses until alternatives are *symbolically* tested,[5] build on the much higher structural complexity of language, man's primary, all-pervasive communicative system. Here lies the apparently unbridgeable difference between language and all other animal 'codes'. The bees' communication dance, decoded by von Frisch, presents at least five handicaps in comparison with human language[6]: fixity of content, invariability of message, reference to one situation only, non-analysability of the message, and unilateralism of its transmission (the dance elicits a behavioural response, not any message in reply). Only in man there exists an ability to project symbolic chains ad libitum; only he possesses in language a tool for freeing individuals from the tyranny of experience.[7]

On second thoughts, however, the symbolic turns out to be quite a complex matter. Even a cursory survey of the literature shows that the widespread interest of social scientists in cultural symbolism goes far beyond the peculiar but too generic phenomenon of the wonderfully creative powers of human language. What lures the sociological curiosity is one specific feature of man's symbolic—the luxuriance of its *figurative* idioms, including the motley variety of *cryptosemantics*: the wealth of hidden, often latent meanings, supporting, or emanating from, a host of situations in social life. Here we leave the specifics of human *signs* and begin to focus on a special type of signs—on symbols proper. Or rather, we remain within the field of semiotics, but on condition that we beware of the virtually *translinguistic* dimension of symbolism (unlike language, symbols are often non-verbal). It is clearly from this broad perspective that Geertz proposes to convert the semiotic approach into the backbone of an 'interpretive theory of culture'.[8]

Of course, the main reason why the symbolic, in this sense, appeals so much to social scientists is the density with which it occurs precisely at the very heart of culture. Symbolic condensation, substitution and displacement—to employ the useful Freudian terms—are exceedingly frequent, and particularly significant, whenever values are involved in culture processes. Symbolism is so to speak the lingua franca of value-orientations. The latter we may define, following Kluckhohn, as explicit or implicit generalized structured conceptions, shaping behaviour, of man's place in the world and man's relation to man.[9]

The general nature of values in culture can be circumscribed by resorting to a few other formal definitions. To begin with, values can be classified according to their

(a) modality (positive or negative values);

(b) content (cognitive, moral, expressional);

(c) intent (instrumental or goal values);

(d) degree of generality (specific or 'thematic' values);

(e) degree of intensity (categorical, preferential, hypothetical or ritualistic values, whether central or peripheral, i.e. influencing vital or less vital behaviours, in large or limited number, both these criteria being measured by the kinds of sanctions applied in case of deviant behaviour);

(f) degree of explicitness;

(g) degree of extent (from individual values to axiological human universals); and

(h) the form of their hierarchical organization.[10]

In the light of these criteria, legitimacy should be classified as a value positive in modality; cognitive, moral or expressional in content, since it is contingent on the social sphere to which the experience of legitimacy applies, e.g., intellectual, political or aesthetic; generally instrumental in intent; thematic in generality; categorical or ritualistic in intensity, while central or peripheral;

and extremely variable in explicitness, extent, and hierarchical structure.

Moreover, values are to be distinguished from such things as attitudes, motivations, needs, ideals and beliefs. *Attitudes* refer, since Allport, exclusively to individuals. *Motivation* does not imply the pursuit of standards. *Needs*, though they sometimes arise from cultural values, are too much of a rephrasing of instincts for allowing confusion with social values. *Ideals* do not demand choice, and *belief*, referring primarily to truth or falsity rather than to good or bad, right or wrong, does not necessarily involve commitment.[11]

Smelser, while accepting Kluckhohn's concept of value-orientation, describes values as 'the most general statements of *legitimate* ends which guide social action', norms being the embodiment of such statements.[12] Seen from this viewpoint, *legitimacy corresponds to the validity dimension in cultural symbolism*. Legitimacy patterns are value-laden sets of culture traits; together, they constitute a kind of unwritten gospels—a 'secular scripture'[13]—underlying the cognitive, practical or expressional conduct of a given group (not necessarily a total society).

As is to be expected, such legitimacy patterns (as detected, for instance, by Weber) presuppose motivational experiences. In terms of the dispositional types discriminated above, legitimacy can be seen as the provider of a bridge between 'pure' motivation, that is, motivations indifferent to standards, and the hierarchical realm of values. In behavioural terms, then, *legitimacy is motivation plus a sense of value-hierarchy*.

Lazarsfeld has tried to classify disposition concepts according to three criteria:

(a) generality-or-specificity (an interest can be directed toward several spheres or to a limited object);
(b) degree of directiveness (an attitude toward or versus a desire for something, the former being passive, the second a drive); and
(c) time perspective (dispositions focused on the future as against dispositions concentrated on the present).

Thus, *opinions* tend to be specific, passive and current; *attitudes*, general, passive and current; *needs*, specific, driving, and current; *expectations*, specific, passive, and future-orientated; *tendencies*, general, passive and future-orientated; *plans*, specific, driving and future-orientated; and *motivations*, general, driving, and rather inclined to bridge the present and the future.[14]

Grosso modo, sentiments of legitimacy, as a dispositional type, seem to present a general, passive and temporally 'bridging' character. This is particularly visible in the political sphere, where the experience of legitimate authority consists in a positive, complying attitude (passivity) towards *several* decisions (generality) spreading throughout a large time-scale (the life of a traditional ruler, the spell of a charismatic leadership, the tenure of a legally held office); but it also applies, with qualifications, to non-political legitimacy. Think of the usual behaviour in matters of artistic taste, for example: legitimate art styles benefit from generalized 'contemplative' approval (i.e. approval covering more than one limited work) stretching in time (the approval concerns the present but persists in the form of aesthetic expectations).

One crucial question emerges here: Is such a dispositional cast of mind permanent, or only historical? In other words, are there, actually or potentially, *other* types of legitimacy-disposition, specific instead of general, present-orientated instead of future-orientated, and, more important still, *driving* rather than passive? I must adjourn the answer. This is precisely one of the central issues to be dealt with in a key province of the sociology of culture: the historical typology of legitimacy patterns.

For the moment, however, let us not go into any details concerning legitimacy value-patterning and its behavioural counterparts, for we still have to be a little more specific about the nature and functioning of social symbolism, as distinct from the basic, generic, structure of language—about *symbolization* as distinct from the general function of *signification*.

On a very abstract plane, the function of social symbolism has been very instructively highlighted by Lévi-Strauss's postulate of a *floating signifier*.[15] His thesis is well known: language, hence meaning, cannot have appeared in human evolution otherwise than suddenly. All of a sudden mankind has passed from a stage where nothing signified to another where everything has a sense. Still, this turning meaningful did not, of course, warrant any further knowledge of the components of the universe. Meaningfulness was a sudden fiat (however lengthy its incubation); knowledge, an infinite step-by-step progress. The order of meaning is since its very inception the realm of discontinuity; the order of knowing is by nature—pace Thomas Kuhn—ruled by continuity. Therefore, in

89

his attempt to understand the world, man always disposes of a 'surplus of signification', to be periodically redistributed by the mythopoetical imagination, so that the recovery of the 'integrity of meaning' becomes precisely the main task of religion, myth and art. The basic function of social symbolism, then, is to reallocate periodically the surplus of signification; to restore meaningfulness to life as a whole.

Before turning to more concrete, less general aspects of symbolization in culture, let us now cast a glimpse at the scholarly route of the symbol concept. In his recent and careful inventory of symbol theory, Sir Raymond Firth[16] begins by noticing that the rationalist temper of the Enlightenment was basically uninterested in the emotional resonances and mystical proclivities of social symbolism, so that the first attempts at a systematic exploration of the latter came with the rise of romanticism. In fact, an outright doctrine of aesthetic symbolism, revelatory in character, and strongly opposed to allegory, was set forth by Goethe in the full-fledged Weimar classicism—a literary movement attacked by the romantics, and at any rate closer to the Enlightenment (being itself a qualified Aufklärung) than to romanticism.

As Gadamer brilliantly demonstrated, in the wake of the subjectivization of the concept of expression that marked the cultural turning-point of the end of the eighteenth century, symbol was far better placed than allegory to become the talisman of art and idealistic philosophy. For one thing, allegory hinged on tradition and was therefore hardly suitable to be taken up by the subjectivistic slant of expressivism (the same trend we met as a keynote of historicism). Symbolism, by contrast, according to a time-honoured religious semantics, was just that type of meaning lying beyond external appearance or sound which did *not* amount to a random choice or creation of a sign but, on the contrary, implied a 'higher' metaphysical connection of visible and invisible—the connection substantiated in the instant and total coincidence of appearance with the Absolute in religious cult.[17] After all, 'symballein' means 'bring together'.

Be that as it may, however, the real *study* of symbolism waited for romanticism. True, nascent classical philology around 1800 flirted with the symbolic interpretation of ancient myths. The great Hellenist and Humboldt's friend, Gottfried Hermann, who combined Winckelmann's passionate love for antiquity with Kant's epistemology, and was a fierce anti-romantic, 'translated' gods into natural forces or moral principles; but this was a passing dalliance not a lifelong passion. The true founding fathers of the analysis of social symbols were genuine romantics. Jacques-Antoine Dulaure (fl. 1805) foreshadowed a behavioural proto-anthropological conception of symbolism, tracing myth into cult. His contemporary, Georg Friedrich Creuzer, stressed the pragmatic significance of symbols both as instruments of learning and as vehicles of mystical experience. Within two generations, after Gotthilf-Heinrich Schubert and Carl-Gustav Carus had pioneered the study of dream symbolism, Bachofen (*Graebersymbolik der Alten*, 1850) came to see myth as the exegesis of symbols (a century later, Lévi-Strauss was to do it the other way round).

Meanwhile, Fustel de Coulanges, Durkheim's master, opened a new and quite seminal path: the *institutional* approach to symbolism. Fustel saw ancient religion, McLennan, marriage customs, Robertson Smith, sacrifice, and Frazer, nature symbols, related to sacred kingship in terms of their social functions within institutional contexts. Shortly afterwards, Durkheim himself consolidated this trend of analysis. Vigorously opposing the romantic idea of *nature* symbolism, he emphasized the role of *society* in the genesis of symbols, cognitive as well as religious, thereby inaugurating a whole line of research, of which Bateson's reading of Iatmül role symbolism, or Fortes and Evans-Pritchard's claims about the functions of African political symbols, were to become classic instances.

Parallel to the gradual transformation of romantic hermeneutics into an incipient sociological approach, there emerged from philosophical quarters an equally fruitful theorizing: Peirce's semiotics, a sophisticate theory and taxonomy of signs. But Peirce's ideas on sign took a long time to gain influence (and, then, like his pragmaticism, which was so impoverished by James, they were distorted, in the rather platitudinous behaviouristic semiotics of a much later theorist, Charles Morris). Well before his papers were collected in book form, psychoanalysis had made a major contribution to the deciphering of cryptic, censored, repressed meaning. Like Peirce but unlike Durkheim, Freud did improve our knowledge of the conceptual operations involved in symbolization —the mechanics of symbolism.

In this regard, Malinowski's collaboration with Ogden and Richards's psychologistic semantics in the 1920s, though producing an interesting typology of sign-referent relations (active, indirect, magic), should be considered as a regression. Malinowski's pragmatic view of symbolism stimulated the healthy concern of the London School of linguistics (J. R. Firth, M. Halliday) with semantic *contexts*, an important aspect of verbal experience, somewhat neglected by the Saussurean linguists of the Prague circle; but, as even a most sympathetic critic like Raymond Firth recognizes, the founder of modern anthropology was unduly hostile to symbolic interpretations resorting to 'hidden realities'[18] and he overstated the conspicuously practical social referent of myth symbolism.

The contrast with Sapir could not be greater, for Sapir deliberately played down the mainly practical-cognitive *referential* symbols in order better to value *condensation* symbols: symbols, that is, defined as 'highly condensed forms of substitutive behaviour for direct expression, allowing for the ready release of emotional tension'.[19] In the Sapirian unabashedly psychological anthropology, condensation symbolism, very often found in ritual, grounds deep on the unconscious, and expresses powerfully emotional and orectic meanings; it is the terse language of feeling and appetite.

Such were, in very broad lines, the main directions of the study of social symbolism before Lévi-Strauss and Victor Turner, the two leading theorists nowadays. I have obviously excluded from the picture major literary critics deeply interested in the symbolic, from Burke to Frye or Barthes, though I wholeheartedly agree with Geertz in seeing their work as a legitimate potential source of inspiration for an anthropological semiotic of culture.[20] The same applies, a fortiori, to the less frivolous part of the proliferation of semiotic research since the 1960s and, in particular, to Hall's proxemics.[21]

I am afraid the mention of two other not so recent prominent symbol theorists—Cassirer and Jung—strikes less positive a note. The former, though he kept at a wholesome remove from the appalling irrationalist excesses of the mainstreams of German philosophy after, or since, Husserl's *Ideen*, is surely responsible in a major way for moving neo-Kantianism away from critical epistemology. His 'philosophy of symbolic forms' was, indeed, as Passmore puts it, the work of a 'recalcitrant metaphysician'.[22] Moreover, for all its grand design (later to some extent trivialized by his disciple, Suzanne Langer), Cassirer's symbology has little to say about the particulars of symbolism, and understandably so:

aiming at turning every dimension of the mind, including science, into a symbol-making agency, it commits itself to generalization rather than specification.[23]

As for Jung, the head of a neo-romantic revival in symbol theory, his breakaway from Freud must be seen as an essentially pre- rather than post-Freudian move. In spite of the limited but real heuristic value of archetypal imagery, Rieff puts a shrewd finger on the truth when he invites us to look at Jung as a fundamentally reactionary scholar, in whose work Protestant theological erudition, achieving a pitiful reversal, comes to attack what once was his proud incentive: critical rationalism. Jung's *cultic* attitude towards religion and culture, his balsamic 'wisdom', his sage-like prose and anti-science furore were but the last afterglows of 'literary humanism in its most vengeful form'[24]—and as such, something that deserves more debunking than commendation. In any event, the man who wrote so many learned disquisitions on such a vast set of symbols and their transformations (as well as on transformation symbols) did envisage symbolism as a healing force, not as an object of critical analysis. It is therefore more than appropriate to take him at his word and look elsewhere for *principles*, rather than simple cues, of discovery and explanation of matters symbolic.

The critical conclusion, up to here, is not very hard to draw. Of the theoretical paths reviewed by Firth four—the institutional, the semiotic, the psychoanalytic and the psycho-anthropological approaches, respectively headed by Durkheim, Peirce, Freud and Sapir—seem to make a lot of sense in the study of social symbolism. Their combination, joining the awareness of institutional contexts and a sophisticate picture of the mechanics of symbolic semiosis to a sharp flair for the elusive ambiguities of the cryptosemantics of symbolism, promises to fare even better. Only one big absence is to be deplored: that of social differentiation and power structure as a source of symbolic strategies,[25] the trend (chiefly of Marxian origin) which ought to be named critique of *ideological* symbolism—a kind of symbolic of great importance, even at the level of several illiterate societies like the African cultures studied by Fortes and Evans-Pritchard.

Let us now cast a closer glance at the functioning of social symbolism. In so doing, we shall kill two birds with one stone, for, while commenting on further insights into symbolization processes, we shall update our discussion of the literature by briefly considering the work of Turner and Lévi-Strauss.

Professor Turner's reflection on symbolism owes many a theme to two of the scholars at whose mention our survey of symbol theory was interrupted, Sapir and Jung. Turner took very seriously Sapir's concern with condensation symbols in his own analysis of the ritual symbolism of the Zambian people, the Ndembu. Unfortunately, the fact that he also set great store by Jung's foggy ideas about the irreducible unknowability of symbols, as distinct from mere signs, did not help clarify the epistemological status of his otherwise highly suggestive theory and hermeneutic of social symbolism. Turner's main work up to now, *The Forest of Symbols*, lives up to the promise of its Baudelairean title by laying down a dense, three-storeyed architecture of symbolic meaning. *Exegetical* meaning corresponds to the level of indigenous interpretation; *operational* meaning, to the effective social use of symbols, as well as to their emotional connotations; *positional* meaning, to the structural relationships of symbols among themselves.[26]

Now, as Dan Sperber[27] pointed out, a symbolic system may work very satisfactorily without being endowed with any full exegesis, not even an 'authentic' one, like jurists say. Our elaborate codes of politeness are a case in point: they often fall short of a full exegetical justification. While we can 'explain' several polite gestures (if only in a survivalist fashion worthy of a Tylor, as when we remember that shaking hands originally derived from a token of friendliness, in so far as extending the right hand naturally precluded hitting the other person), many other acts lack similar, or any, rationalizations. Furthermore, native exegesis itself, as much as the symbol's use, needs interpretation.[28] Unless we stop like Jung before the miranda of myth, and forgo interpretation (after some archetypal translating) in the name of an awesome respect for the mysteries of the Unknown, we are forced to grant that exegesis and use—especially in its Sapirian connotative, emotional over-tones—telescope each other without ever forming a univocal criterion of intelligibility (however polysemic its raw material). The obvious way out seems to lie in the hands of psychoanalysis, which, in principle, subjects both use and exegesis to an interpretation resorting to the unconscious and its laws—to the unconscious as an extra-symbolic reality, not, as for the Jungians, as a mythopoetic reservoir. This, however, claims Sperber, suggestive as it may in turn be, boils down to merely taking an association *to be explained* (that of symbolism with unconscious drives) for the explanation itself. Pointing to the links between the symbolic and the libido is perfectly legitimate, and heuristically fruitful, only it does not in the least provide a validation for our would-be explanatory interpretations. 'The cryptological view [that is, Turner's] posits at the outset a set of symbols as given in a culture; the Freudian view posits at the outset a set of interpretations as given in the unconscious. Both leave the logic of the relationships (symbol, interpretation) largely indeterminate or even posit this indeterminateness as an intrinsic characteristic of symbolism.'[29]

The only direction left is, therefore, *positional* meaning. In other words, Turner's cryptology calls for Lévi-Strauss's structural analysis. In the structural analysis of a complex symbolic system such as myth, each of the symbolic units (mythemes) never carries meaning by itself but only in virtue of its opposition (homological or not) to at least one other unit. Moreover, the oppositions themselves may belong to *several* domains (culinary, cosmological, sociological, etc.), not to just one, as it often happens in vulgar psychoanalysis.

Above all, oppositions may split into further oppositions—and, in the process, they may be inverted. Completion of the structural interpretation of (op)positional meanings frequently proceeds by detecting symbolic values which are the exact reverse of the symbol under scrutiny (and since 'mythical thought derives from the realization of certain oppositions and tends to progressively mediating between them', inversions most often express the ambivalence of culture toward the predicament of man or of the world; thus, in Lévi-Strauss's own early example, the inverted motives of assertion and denial of autochthony in the Oedipus myth[30]—the hero's lameness, a link with the Tellus Mater, and his murdering the Sphinx, a chthonic monster apud Marie Delcourt—dialectically highlight each other).

Therefore Lévi-Strauss, while providing a systematic model for what Turner was later to call positional meaning, innovates in analysis by adding at least two elements:

(a) the concept of levels of *reduction* of logical oppositions within symbolic structures;
(b) the recognition of the phenomenon of systematic symbolic *inversion*.

Previous analyses of symbolism used to classify their data by dint of the criteria of similarity and contiguity (just remember Frazer's two forms of magic, homeopathic and contagious: the former confusing resemblance, the second, vicinity with causality). By adding the 'negative' criteria of reducible opposition and inversion, structuralism vastly enhances the interpreter's ability to find meaningful relations of sundry semantic provenances.

According to Sperber, the structural study of myth—the most sophisticated symbol hermeneutic to date—is precisely this, though no more than this: a highly rewarding heuristic.[31] As for its explanatory powers, Sperber remains sceptical. For one thing, he refuses to accept Lévi-Strauss's lofty indifference towards the question of whether the structural interpretation ultimately amounts to the reality (however unconscious) of natives' minds or to a simple product of the structuralist's look. Above all, he rejects the structuralist claim to a semiotic status analogous to that enjoyed by linguistic analysis. The structural signification of myth, argues Sperber, is far from constituting a 'language', since the units of mythical meaning are never presented as stable coded pairs of signifiers/signified able to compose 'sentences' according to the rules of a generative grammar.[32] In sum, just as Turner's search for *hidden* meaning fails in the end to qualify as an explanatory theory of symbolism, so does Lévi-Strauss's ordering of *absent* meaning, whose principle comes down to an organization, *not* an encoding, of information. An intellectual bricolage, symbol structuralism is not, pace Lévi-Strauss, a true semiology.

However, Sperber is only too glad to demonstrate that structuralist semiotics, however powerful as an heuristic device, is theoretically self-deluding because if we believe him *every* semiotic approach to symbolism is bound to be mistaken. Symbols, he says, are not at all 'meanings'; if they mean, it is only in the same general, useless sense as sentences, or objects, also mean—a sense which obviously tells us nothing at all about the specificity of symbolism. For Sperber, symbols do not stand for anything else. Rather, they are the special products of a mental device coupled to the conceptual mechanism, and deeply involved in the vicissitudes of the *cognitive*, not the semiotic, process.

This idea, with which we shall end our instant journey into the history of symbol theory, is certainly worth a moment of attention. Sperber's elegant theorization unfolds in two basic moves.[33] First, it describes symbol construction negatively, by contrasting it with the building of a grammar:

(a) While observable linguistic data, deriving from auditory perception, form a class of distinct percepts, symbolic data do not form a similar class—they just derive from any perceptual source.

(b) While linguistic data, as elements of a verbal grammar, necessarily belong to a given language to the exclusion of the others, symbolic data do not belong to any set exclusive of other sets.

(c) Whilst multilingualism is a permanent possibility in the life of an individual, who can always internalize further verbal grammars, there is no analogous multisymbolism: symbolic data, whatever their origin, always integrate themselves into a single system within a given individual.

(d) On the other hand, language-learning, however multiplied, is always, in each grammar's case, soon over for the individual. In symbolic-learning, on the contrary, no such thing happens: the learning of symbolism, because it is a cognitive not a code phenomenon, is a life-long process. In every individual, language-learning knows beginnings and thresholds; symbolic-learning does not.

Then, with the help of modern semantics, a distinction is drawn between symbolic, 'encyclopaedic' and semantic knowledge. Encyclopaedic knowledge is about the world; it expresses itself by means of synthetic propositions (e.g. 'Lions are dangerous', or 'William is the husband of Hilda'). Semantic knowledge is about categories; it employs analytic propositions (e.g., 'Lions are animals', or 'A bachelor is a single person'). Most of our categories of thought comprehend semantic and encyclopaedic aspects. Some, however, are purely semantic (e.g., 'now', 'this/that'); others, purely encyclopaedic (proper names). Now, semantic knowledge about each category is finite; encyclopaedic knowledge, potentially infinite. It is possible to know all about the *meaning* of the word 'lion' but clearly impossible to know everything about lions as beings.

Symbolic knowledge, like encyclopaedic knowing, is potentially infinite. The more encyclopaedic knowledge is enriched, the more symbolism gets richer: for symbolization is a parasite of our grasp of the world. Unlike encyclopaedic knowledge, however, symbolism is not articulate so as to accept implications free of contradictions.

If a Dorze peasant keeps guarding his livestock on fast days, even when Dorze symbolism tells that leopards, being 'good Christians', do obey the religious calendar, it is because he believes *both* that leopards religiously fast in special weekdays *and* that they naturally attack livestock during the whole week. In much the same way, Christians believe that Mary was a virgin and nevertheless bore a son. In encyclopaedic knowledge, no matter how spurious, contradictions are, as a rule, avoided; in symbolism, they are ignored. Symbolic knowledge indulges in a systematic relaxation of logical constraints.

Symbolism is ultimately not about analytical categories nor things; it simply takes encyclopaedic knowledge as a means to express something else. A meta-encyclopaedia (*not* a meta-language), it puts, as it were, encyclopaedic knowledge *in quotes*. That is why there is no utterance which is not, in principle, capable of turning symbolic. I feel tempted to add: like the aesthetic, according to the Czech semioticist, Jan Mukarowsky,[34] the symbolic is no special region of reality; rather, it is the product of a certain way of looking at anything (which does not preclude some social agencies from institutionalizing such a way of looking—hence the existence of the arts and the art world). Nothing *is*, in itself, symbolic; everything can *become* so (but again, there are social agencies institutionally engaged in the production and dispensation of symbolism).

So much for the nature of symbolism; but what about its *function*? Sperber thinks that symbolicity is an effect of the idiosyncrasies of the intellect. The conceptual mechanism never works in vain. So, when the mind finds itself at a loss to establish the cognitive relevance of its object, it turns to itself. As information is brought under conceptual focus, the intellect mobilizes at the same time the previous knowledge that the newcomer may enrich upon or alter, as well as the analytical rules of 'validation', i.e. of linking the implications of the new information to previous knowledge; but whenever this double operation of remembrance and logical connection fails, symbolism takes over: the information becomes a prey to the symbolizing power of the mind, which feeds its evocational drive on encyclopaedic knowledge without nevertheless obeying its methods of organization. In short, the inputs of symbolism are the defective outputs of the conceptual mechanism. Sperber resorts to Neisser's cognitive psychology: when a sequential process fails, a parallel process is triggered and the normal order of cognition is inverted. Symbolism thrives on the withdrawal of cognition.

At the outset of his brilliant critique of symbol theory, Sperber blamed the ubiquitous *residualism* of thinking on symbolism. Symbolic thought was indeed often conceived of as either the mental minus the rational (Frazer, Lévy-Bruhl), or the semiotic minus the code (cryptologies, structuralism). Ironically, however, his own position is not altogether so different from these unsatisfactory theses. As Maurice Bloch was quick to remark, in presenting symbolism as the result of the mind's turning to irrationality whenever its cognitive efforts are thwarted Sperber places himself very close to Frazer.[35] There is indeed ground enough to wonder whether Sperber himself does not lapse into a new residualism. Does he not see symbolism as the cognitive minus cognition? In this case the cognitive symbol theory would be no more than an avatar of the paternalistic irrationalist conception of the symbolic—and Sperber, a kind of Lévy-Bruhl minus ethno-centricity.

On the other hand, the image of symbolism as a parasite of the failure of cognition, a process triggered by the conceptual mechanism whenever it is frustrated in its cognitive ambitions, smacks strongly—and paradoxically—of intellectualism. It portrays too cerebral a phenomenon. The emotional richness of symbolism, so perceptively grasped from Durkheim to Sapir (not to mention earlier theorizations), does not enter the picture. Nor does the dimension whose lack among symbol theories we noticed above: the recognition that symbolism may serve as a power strategy in social life. In both these crucial points, Sperber's cognitive theory—which, despite the avowed unsubstantiation of its psycho-logical hypotheses, sounds surely suggestive from an heuristic point of view—is rather regressive.

However, let us not finish on such a gloomy note. For a sociology of culture, the great interest of Sperber's 'cognitive' symbol theory lies in a revival of the symbol/society theme—a crucial subject, somewhat neglected ever since Lévi-Strauss, turning Durkheim upside down, declared the mind to be a prius to society (a logical, not an ontological one; but a prius all the same).

In Sperber's terms, in so far as symbolic propositions contain data which the individual could not cognitively organize nor assimilate to the shared ways of communication, they became the food of personal fantasy; but in looking for the most coherent possible treatment for the heterogeneous symbolic information with which they confront themselves, individuals find that their 'evocational fields' tend to overlap and be shared. Cultural symbolism thrives on this process.

As Sperber[36] stresses, the 'evocational fields' determined by the symbolization process differ greatly from one society to another, and vary with social change. They also hinge on a 'commonality of interest', though not of opinion (individuals are left free for completing at will the evocations), roughly amounting to the particular 'points of view' adopted in each society. Apparently, we are not far from the old concept of ethos.

In any event, such an account of the links between individual evocation and cultural symbolic is not a model of clarity; but these evocational fields are, I suggest, a natural subject of a kind of semiotic analysis unmentioned in Sperber's book: the semiotics *of signification* (as distinct from the semiotics of communication), whose conceptual armoury lies not in the Saussurean and Chomskyan linguistics but rather in Peirce's classification of signs.[37]

As we know, Peirce distinguishes the *symbol*, an essentially *conventional* sign, from both the *index* and the *icon*. Indices are signs defined by their *contiguity* in regard to that which they represent; icons, signs that *resemble* the signified. Now the evocational fields of symbolism, while partly provided by social institutions (like religious agencies), are for a large part, *not* conventional, in which case they partake of the nature of symbols (in the Peircean sense) *and of indices*, that is to say of signs whose meaning, *unintentionally* produced (most indices are *natural symptoms*, not artificial signals), stems from any given (social) situation. From Peirce's viewpoint, our cultural symbols would never be just 'symbols'—they would be indices as well, and sometimes, as sheer symptoms, *just* indices.

In linguistic theory, *denotation* is that which, in the semantic value of a term, is common to all the speakers of a given language, whilst *connotations*, in the plural, represent all that the same term can evoke in, or suggest to, each one of the speakers.[38] Connotations are therefore the denizens of the land of social differentiation: for, since they vary from an individual to another, they do so to a large extent along what most differentiates them among themselves—and that is, apart from biological factors, their role in social structure and their place in social stratification.

The various 'evocational fields' determined by man's universal symbolic capacity are composed of cultural connotations, verbal or not. To that extent, symbols are Peircean symbols/indices explainable by means of a sociosemiotic alert to socially determinate meaning. Just as the linguist cannot help tracing the main lines of social differentiation, from classes to age groups, whenever he looks for the connotations (as distinct from the denotation) of words, so the sociologist of culture, recognizing in symbolism the mother language of social values, commits himself to seeking the index-meaning of collective symbolism, beneath or beyond its conventional, 'official' meaning. And here we may depart from Sperber while at the same time agreeing with him: for if, on the one hand, *this* kind of hidden meaning of symbolism *is clearly semiotic* (no matter how much it be the product of a collapse of the cognitive process) on the other hand, this meaning is definitely not a code-paired meaning ruled by generative grammars.

The Italian semioticist, Eco, has recently defined connotation, from a translinguistic standpoint, as the set of cultural units *institutionally* suggested by any given signifier.[39] I cannot agree with such a limitation—it would be fatal to the interests of a *critical* sociology of culture. Fortunately, we possess excellent examples of a less restrictive idea of connotative meaning. Suffice it to think of Panofsky's iconology,[40] a discipline, in his own words, ruled by Peirce's concept of content: a meaning that 'shows itself through' (like the cultural significance of works of art) without nevertheless being exhibited.

As a rueful postscript, let me just point out a remarkable study unfortunately not yet available at the time of my writing this chapter: *Symbol and Theory* by John Skorupski. Taking his cue from a celebrated vindication of intellectualist theories of myth and symbol—Robin Horton's claim that African systems of religious belief should be viewed, just as in Frazer, as theoretical attempts at the explanation of natural processes and events—Dr Skorupski draws a convincingly sharp contrast between such a *literalist* account of mythical thought and what he calls the *symbolist* approach. The latter, illustrated by Durkheim, Lévy-Bruhl or Evans-Pritchard, always separates the literal meaning of myth and religious symbol from their supposed symbolic sense, while at the same time relating this symbolic meaning to underlying social structures. In so doing, 'symbolist' theorists of mythical thought set little store by the surface semantics of religious belief—and this is precisely what Prrofessor Horton, in a series of essays dating back from the late 1960s, takes them to task for.

However, neither in his criticism of some serious flaws in the intellectualist, Hortonian position, nor in his general preference of the latter over the symbolist one, does Skorupski balk at admitting that the 'symbolist usage of relating symbol to social structure' has often been at least a very fruitful heuristics. Moreover, it is also one whose explanatory counterpart would presumably owe next to nothing to the intellectualist approach, for at most, we would be dealing with two distinct sets, or dimensions, of social symbols: on the one hand, myths qua pieces of cosmology; on the other, myths as cathetic/cathartic phenomena. It would be rather impoverishing for anthropology if, in order to rescue the former mythical dimension of a prolonged and unjustified neglect, it ended up by dropping the probing of the other. In short, perhaps we can, and must, have *both* Horton *and* Durkheim—both the intellectualist and the symbolist accounts of symbol.

(1976)

6 Althusser, the humanist malgré lui (a polemic fragment)

For all his boastful obsession with scientific Theory (with a superstitious, symbolist-like capital letter), Althusser and the Althusserians denote an appalling unfamiliarity with most of the landmarks in the philosophy of science. To be sure, Althusserianism contains references to the work of a few *historians* of science (Cavaillès, Koyré), to Canguilhem or Bachelard (the father of the notion, rather hypostatized nowadays, of 'problematic'), and lately, somewhat grudgingly, to Kuhn's psychology of research (after all, the discontinuity between paradigms was asserted by Kuhn immediately before the not dissimilar myth of the 'coupure épistémologique'). But Mill and Mach, Carnap, Hempel and Nagel, Duhem and Popper, Braithwaite and Lakatos, Feyerabend, Harré and Putnam, just as the 'humanists' Polanyi, Toulmin, Gadamer and Habermas, are conspicuously absent from the writings of the school (we are not asking for adhesion to any line but just for awareness of current debates). The scholastic 'course of philosophy for scientists' taught by Althusser at the École Normale Supérieure in 1967 (*Philosophie et philosophie spontanée des savants*) is by no means an improvement: it discusses Lenin but not the Vienna circle or its intimate enemies; once more, the superior knowledge of Dialectic condescends to lecture science and its incurable blindness before the canonic relations between theory and praxis. . . . Even a sympathizer such as Therborn—himself poorly informed about critical epistemology—admits that Althusser's discussions of science 'have never explored the problem of verification or empirical validation' (*Science, Class and Society*, p. 61). In fact, Therborn is slightly mistaken. The lack of a validity theory in Althusser is no omission: it is the product of a deliberate denial of the whole basic epistemological issue. In *Reading Capital* (pp. 52–9), the master sovereignly decrees that the classical problem of knowledge is simply unreal and that any philosophy that finds intriguing the relation between the object of knowledge and the real one is sheer ideology, promptly to be dismissed. Since 'theoretical practice is . . . its own criterion' it validates by itself its own products. Ergo, epistemologists and philosophers of science are idle ideologists, who insist on disregarding the happy fact that the 'knowledge effect' relies on the ability of the established sciences to legitimize their own findings and results through 'forms of proof' answerable to no other authority than theirs. Thus Althusser slyly utilizes the institutional dimension of science—the fact that the ascertaining of scientific truth is a specialized social process and not a direct reflection of a metaphysically asserted external reality—to explain away Reichenbach's 'context of justification'. Indeed, the Althusserian definition of science as a knowledge-producing practice which grasps the essence of the 'real-concrete' through a 'concrete-in-thought', itself the end-product of an active 'problematic', i.e. a 'system of questions' which relates concepts in view of the knowledge-production (*Reading Capital*, esp. pp. 34–52, 62–70), tends patently to dissolve justification issues in a overwhelming 'context of discovery'. In *real*, as distinct from Althusserian, science, the obvious *technical* immanence of justification to each constituted science does not in the least abolish the critical and regulative role of *logical* criteria (e.g., the deductive-nomological model) *common* to every scientific endeavour, and, as general formal rules of explanation and testing, in no sense immanent to any particular scientific field. This had nothing to do whatsoever with the alleged 'bourgeois epistemology' caricatured by Althusser: an empiricism which conceives of knowledge as a 'direct' relation between real things and thought objects, thereby engendering an 'ideological question of guarantees of the possibility of knowledge' (*Reading Capital*, p. 56). The Althusserian onslaught on bourgeois empiricism is pathetically redundant: being only the consequence of a dogmatic ignorance of Popperian and post-Popperian epistemology, it can only reach, through a laborious smugness, a blatantly foregone conclusion. In no way it disposes of the *real* problem—that of validation. Substituting for the context of justification a puny, mythical 'discourse of the proof' (*op. cit.*, pp.

67–8), Althusser pronounces by philosophical fiat a kind of immaculate conception of valid knowledge. We have here a prismatic multiplication of Spinoza's 'veritas norma sui'. Like Spinoza, Althusser brazenly ignores the vexing question of the necessary *logical* transcendence of the criterion of truth, but unlike Spinoza, unfortunately, his ultimate aim is not a beatific unio mystica but the legitimation of philosophy as 'théorie de la pratique théorique'—and, in his own words, the demonstration of the scientificity of Marxism (*Eléments d'Autocritique*, p. 105). Therefore, the rejection of critical epistemology in the form of a general philosophy of science or logic of scientific research leads him, willy-nilly, to a philosophy evacuated of any real *critical* import—and all the more ready to perform futile scholastic acrobatics, like the 'structuralization' of the Marxist concept of causality. The contradiction between the denial of general criteria of scientificity and the claim that Marxist philosophy is the (general) theory of 'theoretical practice', i.e. of science, did not escape Althusser's Marxist critics: for instance, the author of the best English monograph on him considers the treatment of science in *For Marx* and *Reading Capital* 'idealist' just on account of such a glaring contradiction (A. Callinicos, *Althusser's Marxism*, pp. 59–60, 72, 88); but contradiction or not, the fact remains that *Althusser allows no room for a critical view of the intrinsic legitimability of scientific knowledge.* In his later 'self-criticism' period, the anti-theoreticist overtones, struggling to conciliate the fetichized idea of autonomous theory with a conception in which Marxism qua philosophy is no longer the theory of all theoretical practice, but again that hackneyed flatus vocis, 'the class struggle in theory' (*Réponse à John Lewis*, p. 11), amounts to no more than verbal tricks: they may placate orthodox Marxist bigotry but they are clamorously insufficient by any other standards. The illiteracy of structural Marxism in matters epistemological remains to the end a stubborn, premeditated ignorance. Ironically, such an anti-criticalism places Althusser in the neighbourhood of his bête noire, Hegel. Hegel's sleight-of-hand elimination of Kant's critical concern with the validity of knowledge, on the threshold of the *Phenomenology of Mind*, was the fateful step which doomed his objective idealism to irrationalism. In much the same way, with Althusser's flippant dismissal of the validity problem in science, Marxism falls below the level of at least three significant, however eventually failed, attempts at epistemological reflexion within the dialectical tradition: early twentieth-century Austro-Marxism, and the rival Italian schools of della Volpe and Geymonat. (Note that anti-Hegelianism was then, among Marxisms, a pledge of concern with critical epistemology—a lost link, whose restoration, in our days, must be credited to della Volpe's former disciple, Colletti.) Althusser's refusal to engage in epistemology is all the more untenable because of his resolute attack on the two great praxistic Marxisms—that of Lukács and that of Gramsci. Denying themselves the appeal to praxis as the ultimate tribunal of knowledge-validation—since praxism is, in their view, nothing but theoretical laxism—the Althusserians lose ipso facto all right to the only extra-scientifical claim recognized in the Marxist tradition. Extolling science instead of praxis, they condemn themselves to what they ostensibly neglect: the critical question of knowledge, which inheres in every genuine theory of science. It is only too just that the most comprehensive survey of the ways modern philosophers look at science, Radnitzky's *Contemporary Schools of Metascience* (significantly, written from the standpoint of the hermeneutic-dialectic tradition), does not even bother to mention, let alone to discuss, Althusser's work. Let no one mistake our criticism of Althusserianism as an objection made out of a preoccupation with 'methodology'. Philosophy of science is far from being method-obsessed. On the contrary: in its hermeneutic line, such as in Gadamer or Habermas, it implies a thorough-going critique of *methodologism*, while Popper's logic of scientific discovery is definitely not method-concerned, but *task-orientated*. On the other hand, in academic practice, Althusserianism has been no more than a tediously pointless deification of 'method'—the inevitable result of fake theoreticism in our age of thesis-monger academiae. Too often, a certain Marxist naîveté takes Althusserianism for a badly needed theoretical refinement—all the more so, because, as Aron has shown in *D'une sainte famille à l'autre: essais sur les marxismes imaginaires* (pp. 107–10), Althusserianism preserves the classic Marxist jargon, with its keywords like 'production' and 'praxis' (pluralized as 'practices'), while making its content less rigid and thereby much more palatable to the delicate taste of the 'agrégés de philo'. The flirtation with structural anthropology and Lacanian psychoanalysis, the resort to a certain bourgeois philosophical ancestry, seem to warrant the broad-mindedness of this science-worshipping Marxism, so at ease in the 'priestly' and mandarinic precincts of the grandes écoles and the university, yet so conformable to the party line (even though it was born in the early 1960s as a rigorist fundamentalism, within a successful intra-CP reaction against Garaudy's humanistic liberalism; Althusserianism was never rebellious, except on behalf of orthodoxy). In reality, however, structuralist Marxism is strikingly parochial in its range of intellectual conversancy. In none of its central concerns does it evince that willingness to take cognizance of non-Marxist thought which singled out the young Lukács, Gramsci in his gaol, and the Frankfurtians alike, and is now patent in Colletti's essays. A typically Parisian ideology, Althusserianism actually reinforces the deplorable propensity of orthodox Marxism to seclude itself sectarianly from other areas of thought by the regrettable inclination of many French social studies to remain provincially unaware of foreign developments in theory and research. In this sense, Althusserianism is not as much the long-expected Marxization of French socialist thinking as a stealthy Parisianization of Marxism. Ultimately, the enshrinement of science and theory in a fetishist Comte-like fashion became, in the early vintage, up to 1967 Althusser (apparently still far more influential than the later, less scientistic, one), a transparent alibi for not practising science at all—at whatever level. Althusserian pseudo-epistemology threatens to keep the Marxist mind as distant from the serious, fruitful labours of a materialistic sociology as possible. It may well replace the old historicist dialectic that, according to Colletti ('Marxism and the dialectic', *NLR* 93), led to the (relative) paralysis of *historical* materialism—a field of research to which, as far as I know, structuralist Marxism never contributed a single mentionable work. Paradoxically, amidst the present vogue of irrationalist Marxisms (as well as non-Marxisms), Althusserianism is likely to retain a large part of its sway, posing more than ever as 'rational', 'objective' revolutionary thinking. Just as the big Communist parties in Italy and France succeed in playing their 'wisdom' against gauchiste adventurism, so structural Marxist scientism fares well against romantic praxism. All the same, the *social* prestige of the former among left-orientated intellectuals does not in the least cancel its blatant theoretical vacuity. Within French extreme-left intelligentsia, Althusserianism may have turned up as a sophistication (and so it was, too, in other countries with a typically underdeveloped Marxist philosophical culture). In strictly intellectual terms, however, it is *nothing but a sophistic*—a sophistic that professes an ambitious legitimization of Marxism as science, yet never broaches the *legitimacy problem in scientific knowledge*: the problem of logico-empirical validation. P. Anderson (*Considerations on Western Marxism*, pp. 65-6) has pinpointed Althusser's manifold debt to Spinoza, which includes even the cardinal notion of 'structural causality', a secularized avatar of the divine 'causa immanens' in the *Ethics*; but in one crucial point Althusserianism does *not* follow Spinoza's metaphysics. One of the latter's central perspectives is indeed its robust cosmocentricity. Baroque art alone, in its lust for the cosmos, proved capable of matching so resolute an anti-anthropocentric thrust as Spinoza's. Even the sham geometry of the great *Ethics* pays homage to this desire (in his case, mystical) to escape the illusions of anthropomorphic knowledge. Now, the science-minded Althusser, however scornful of humanisms, wholly jeopardizes his claim for objectivity as he refuses to engage in the decisive problem of knowledge, *the true seat of de-anthropomorphization*. As long as they deny the epistemological issue, the Althusserians will remain far behind Popper or even Piaget in regard to the demolition of anthropomorphic theories of knowledge. Indeed they will be, supreme irony, in the company, which is anathema to them, of 'humanists' like Schutz, Polanyi or Toulmin—the very tenants of 'anthropomorphic (ir)rationalism'.

A comprehensive and devastating exposure of Althusser's *philosophical* blunders, especially in relation to empiricism, has been put forward by Leszek Kolakowski in the Socialist Register of 1971; but there can be also at least two other charges, each fraught with paradox. The first was subtly suggested by the late George Lichtheim (in his *From Marx to Hegel*), who hinted at the curious kinship between the over-concern of Althusserianism (via the 'overdetermination' idea) with the uniqueness of the historical individual and . . . historicism, an official bête noire of the school. This might be the virtual *historicist*-malgré-lui charge. The other is the one I have tried to sketch—that Althusser, 'le farouche antihumaniste', is at bottom an inveterate humanist malgré lui.

(1976)

7 A Marxisant Dilthey: Habermas and the epistemology of 'critical theory'

The programme of critical theory can be read on the threshold of the very gospel of the school, the *Dialektik der Aufklärung* (1947): the business of critical theory is *the self-criticism of the enlightenment* (not of course of the 'epochal' Enlightenment, but of a much more comprehensive enlightened *reason*, ranging from ancient magic to modern science, of which eighteenth-century progressism represents only the first global legitimation). The founding leaders of the school—Max Horkheimer, the young Herbert Marcuse, Theodor W. Adorno—were all Jewish intellectuals as strongly committed to *utopian* and *soteriological* thought as their fellow-Marxist, Ernst Bloch. The closing chapter of Adorno's witty and insightful collection of aphorisms, *Minima Moralia* (1951) defines philosophy as 'the attempt to consider everything from the viewpoint of redemption'.

However, since the beginning, hope and salvation became for these thinkers less affirmative forces in the struggle of social man than the victims of a inexorable historical curse; for, as they see it, enlightened reason, which once was at one with freedom, turned into the very opposite of human liberty and happiness. The empire of modern science and technology achieved, to be sure, a rationalization of the world; but, as Weber understood, this triumph of reason has been the victory of merely *instrumental* reason, divorced from any ethical *telos*—and by the same token, prone to the *domination*, and not at all the redemption, of mankind. Thus, man and nature have been enslaved by a maddened reason—a sleepless, monster-breeding reason, a child, not of the hopeful Enlightenment that once drew Goya's 'sueño de la razón', but rather of Chesterton's wise warning: 'a madman is one who lost everything, except reason'.

In depicting such a malignant reason as the major factor in modern Western culture, the Frankfurtians were influenced by decadentist Kulturkritik; one has only to think of Karl Kraus, the Vienna Belle Epoque essayist, for whom the press, originally a weapon of social enlightenment, transformed itself in an instrument of imbecilization. On the whole, as T. Perlini, the Lukács expert, suggests, Frankfurtian Kulturpessimismus personified a sort of rationalization of expressionist culture, a philosophical sublimation of Angst und Urschrei, the expressionist desperate pathos before the crumbling of 'christian-bourgeois' (K. Loewith) civilization.

The main source of the critical theorists' philosophical idiom is Hegel. In Hegel, indeed, in his brilliant odyssey of the mind, the *Phänomenologie des Geistes*, Horkheimer and Adorno found the grounding concepts both of their dialectical method and of their obsessive concern with the Dr Jekyll-and-Mr Hyde nature of scientific reason.

For Hegel already, the Enlightenment embodied the pure intellect, bound to perform an *abstract* negation, unable to reach the blissful stage of the final reconciliation between Geist and world. Both in the *Phänomenologie* (ch. III) and in the second part of his *Logik* (logic of the essence), the intellect (Verstand) is essentially a method of *separation* and of establishing *formal* relationships; it is the bearer of a homogeneously mathematical picture of being. The intellect always operates as *analytical* reason, feeding on division; and, more important, such an Occam's razor, unfit to achieve dialectical synthesis, cannot but finish by destroying itself. Thus absolute enlightened freedom, the intellect as the French Revolution, entailed in the end (says the *Phänomenologie*) its very contrary—the Jacobin tyranny. Left to itself, the Hegelian intellect is so to speak an unhappy antithesis; it is doomed to deny its very aims, that only *post*-Enlightenment reason (Vernunft) can attain, through a superior synthesis. Now it is precisely the comfort of this ultimate, soothing synthesis, that the Frankfurt émigrés have never experienced. Unlike their master Hegel, they have never encountered any redeeming pax dialectica.

What is crucial for us, in all this tragic saga of enlightened reason, is not its philosophy of history but rather its conception of knowledge; and here, unfortunately, we find still another powerful version of irrationalism, under the usual form of a strongly pejorative idea of science. Horkheimer and Adorno's critical theory, it goes without saying, does not present itself as an irrationalism. Quite the contrary: it takes pride in its attacks on irrationalist strongholds, like Heidegger's 'fundamental ontology'. Perhaps the liveliest part of Adorno's *Negative Dialektik* (1966, I) is the assault of the concept against the mystifying puns and the solemn pathos of ontological Denken—a vocationally supralogical 'thought'. Even Horkheimer's nostalgia for the classical logos, in his *Eclipse of Reason* (1947), does not betray any sympathy towards the traditional mainsprings of anti-rational thinking; instead, the polemic against modern, barely formal or instrumental reason goes side by side with the praise for early, classical, 'substantive' rationalism—not of irrationalism.

Yet, when all is said, the fact remains that the very idea of a *critical* science is, for this enlightenment plunged in self-criticism, a *contradictio in adjecto*. Being sheer 'technical performance' (*Dialektik der Aufklärung*), unconscious mythical anxiety in the extreme, science can never aspire to self-understanding. Lucio Colletti (1969) has admirably tracked down the ancestry of the Frankfurtian disparagement of scientific self-knowledge. First and foremost, there is *L'Evolution créatrice* and all the Bergsonian reduction of science to practical activity; but Bergson's irrationalism was absorbed via the bible of Western Marxism: Lukács's 1923 *History and Class Consciousness*.

As P. Hamilton (1974, p. 56) has clearly pointed out, Lukács's epoch-making book is the source of a fatal shift in the concept of science—*for Lukács replaces the critical conception of the ideological in science by the conception that science as such is ideology*. Moreover, Colletti seems again fundamentally right in connecting this shift to other ominous Lukácsian intellectual moves: for in *History and Class Consciousness*, Lukács illegitimately conflates Marxian *historical* alienation, defined by a specific social context in *Capital*, and Hegelian *epistemological* alienation, whereby subject and object are separated in the process of knowing. Thus, as Lukács himself later commented, 'a socio-historical problem was transformed into an ontological problem'.

What was the main consequence of this idealistic conflation? A most dangerous one, since science, turned into mere ideology, came to be viewed as a mere institution of bourgeois culture (Colletti,

1973, pp. 292-3); and in so far as the scientific-technological complex is said to characterize 'industrial society' in general, the social target of critical theory becomes no longer specific social structures *but industrial society as such*. Industrial, or techno-logical, society and, of course, its own 'mass culture' are indeed the usual subject-matter of Adornian unknowing but highly spurious mixture of technologism and culturalism, just as they are the bête noire of Marcuse's (1964) romantic Great Refusal. That Adorno was also an often truly illuminating music and literary critic does not in the least alter the fact that his macro-sociology has shaky foundations, chiefly related, as we have just noticed, to irrationalistic epistemology; nor does his ambivalence regarding empirical sociology (Jay, 1973, ch. 7), an ambivalence which witnesses the uneasiness with which 'critical theory' always dealt with science (although we ought to acknowledge, in this connection, the happy exception of the collective work *Studies in Prejudice*).

Compared to that of the senior members of the school, the work of Jürgen Habermas shows both a subdued version of the utopian/pessimist Stimmung and a more sober assessment of science. In Habermas, the expressionist apocalyptical mood lurking underneath Horkheimer and Adorno's catastrophic vision of history gives place to a quieter, *epistemological, rather than directly 'soteriological'*, frame of mind. With him, critical theory, forsaking its morbid and traumatic fascination for the eclipse of reason, begins to contemplate *salvation through knowledge*. What perverted enlightenment has damaged, Habermas's 'emancipatory knowledge' sets out to restore. Kulturpessimismus changes itself into gnoseological optimism, as confident in the healing powers of 'reflection' as is Althusser in the promised land of Theory.

On the other hand, however, *epistemology itself becomes with Habermas a sort of sublimated soteriological utopia*. The quest for the determination of 'knowledge-constitutive interests', grounded as it is in the demotion of natural science as a paradigm of valid knowledge, springs from the wish to legitimate a humanized and humanizing kind of episteme, a form of knowing that might be the vehicle of human happiness.

In this sense, Habermasian epistemology may be said to be the heir to the neo-idealistic critique of science. The way reflection, the highest type of knowledge in Habermas's threefold classification, stands against the 'objectivism' of science explicitly echoes the

Leitmotiv of Husserl's *Krisis der europäischen Wissenschaften*. The difference lies in the Marxism of Habermas, to whom the phenomenological suppression of positivistic objectivism is tainted with a fatal birth-flaw: it still endorses the *contemplative* ideal of knowledge. Husserl wanted to rescue science from objectivism by a return to the culture-formative powers of 'true theory'; but, in so doing, despite his acknowledgment of a life-world underneath objective knowledge, he attached 'the expectation of practical efficacy', the hope of a renewal of the ethical meaning of science, to the 'freeing of knowledge from interest' (Habermas 1968, p. 306). In other words, phenomenology wrongly tried to regenerate science by a repristination of theoretical authenticity, when the real need of a critical epistemology was (and has so remained) to deepen the understanding of the theory/praxis relationship.

The Marxist phenomenologist, John O'Neill (1972, ch. 15), has tried to acquit phenomenology of Habermas's charge of theoreticism by a curious counter-attack. He argues that reflexivity, the cardinal virtue of Habermasian social knowledge, should be seen as 'institution rather than as transcendental constitution' (as is the case with Habermas's knowledge-constitutive interests). The trouble is that O'Neill's position rests on Merleau-Ponty's 'wordly' phenomenology, not on Husserlian orthodoxy. As everybody knows, Merleau-Ponty took Husserl's Lebenswelt and deprived it from its transcendental framework. His was a phenomenology without Husserl's second, decisive *epoche*. The result can be richer and more colourful to the sociologist's eyes; but unfortunately it is a result obtained at the expense of cognitive rigour. The transcendental viewpoint of Husserl or Habermas may be a bad critical filter; all the same, it is at least an evidence for their *attempt* to cope with the problem of cognitive validity and legitimacy. Compared to it, the French existentialist-phenomenological plunge into the world seems a blind move, an a-critical acceptance of the immediacy of the 'vécu' as a reliable source of knowledge. The fact that Merleau-Ponty as an individual was no conservative does not change anything in this respect. The real issue is: does his work, by detranscendentalizing phenomenology, provide us with true criteria of cognitive legitimacy? If not, his brilliantly suggestive incarnated psychology can seduce blatantly humanistic sociologists like O'Neill—but it can scarcely give them a solid argument against Habermas's epistemology.

According to the latter, there are three types of science, each of them based on one major knowledge interest. Empirical analytical sciences have a *technical* interest; historical interpretive sciences spring from *practical* interests; and systematic, critically orientated, sciences of action, like economics, sociology and politics, are inspired by *emancipatory* knowledge interests. Of all these sciences, only the sciences of action have self-reflection as their method. The three major knowledge interests, technical, practical and emancipatory, are respectively linked to three means of social organization: work, language and power. Hence the three scientific domains: *information*, aiming at the expansion of technical control in work; *interpretation*, ensuring the orientation of action through language within shared traditions; and *analysis*, freeing consciousness from ideologically covered power.

We can discern three main modes of thought as capable of accounting for the dynamics of each scientific field and its related category of knowledge: information, in the empirical sciences, follows the rules of Popper's logic of scientific discovery; interpretation, in the historical interpretive sciences, has been theorized by Gadamer's hermeneutics; finally, analysis, in the action sciences, complies with the epistemological model drawn by Freud's depth psychology. (In fact, in his *opus magnum, Knowledge and Human Interests*, Habermas studies also in detail several other major thinkers. Thus Peirce would figure beside Popper as a chief codifier of the nomothetic empirical sciences, and Dilthey, the father of hermeneutics, beside Gadamer; while Marx is essential to Habermas's (1971, p. 9) own conception of the role of psychoanalysis, the young Hegel provides him with the socio-cultural traid work/language/power, and from Fichte he takes the very concept of interest in connection with self-reflection.)

Knowledge interests enjoy a Kantian *transcendental* status in so far as they are constitutive of scientific object domains; but they are also *empirical* in as much that they derive from mankind's natural history (Habermas, 1971, p. 21). Nevertheless, precisely as 'invariants', as deep-seated drives related to the history of the species, the knowledge interests are much more a subject-matter for a philosophical anthropology (one less idealistic than, for instance, Cassirer's) than a proper object of any sociology of knowledge (ibid., p. 8).

Shortly before *Knowledge and Human Interests*, in *Zur Logik der Sozialwissenschaften* (1967), Habermas's epistemology tried to bridge philosophy and sociological theory. The *Logik* makes no use of the Fichtean-Hegelian terminology of *Erkenntnis und Interesse* but it already plays the idea of sociology as reflexive (psycho) analysis against structural-functionalist behaviourism, which was then, to a European mind, the dominant trend of American widely influential social science.

Starting from Rickert's celebrated opposition between Kultur- and Naturwissenschaften, the essay blames the Parsonian postulate of a basic agreement between the motives of social action and the institutionalized values of a given society for 'impoverishing the concept of tradition'. From the standpoint of Geisteswissen-schaften's problematic, Parsons's theory means to Habermas a regressive step; and so he turns next to show how verstehende sociology surpasses these functionalist shortcomings, underlining that Schütz's phenomenology focuses first on that which Parsons's systemic vision keeps in the shade: the role of intersubjectivity in social behaviour. However, despite the warmth of his treatment of phenomenological sociology, which allows itself even laudatory references to the outspoken irrationalism of a Garfinkel or a Cicourel, Habermas considers Schütz guilty of a typical idealistic sin: the lack of a *linguistic* concept of intersubjective com-munication.

This deficiency compels the Habermasian *Logik* to exchange the Husserlian heritage for Wittgenstein's linguistic philosophy. Yet, in the end, writes Habermas, even Wittgenstein will not do, since his language-worlds are closed within themselves, while a full sense of intersubjectivity *in actu* presupposes a philosophy of tradition *as translation*, and hence of contact between different *open* linguistic universes. Here, Gadamer's hermeneutics supplies what is missing in the Wittgensteinian perspective; but hermeneutics must in turn be corrected by the lesson of Freud, for transcultural interpretation must never forget that language is *also* a means of domination and a living record of the stigmata of repression.

Now analysis, says Habermas (1967, ch. IV, p. 1), approvingly quoting A. C. MacIntyre (1958), is purely interpretative; it has nothing to do with causal explanation. . . . If the *Logik* began with Rickert, its concluding paragraphs seem closer to Dilthey: what therapy as reflection interprets and understands, it simply does not even bother to explain. Emancipatory knowledge does not in the least aspire to the condition of logico-empirical explanation.

In his very illuminating introduction to the fourth German edition of *Theory and Practice* (1971), Habermas returns to his threefold typology of knowledge. This time, however, two kinds of *science*—the empirical-analytical type, in the form of 'causal explanations or conditional predictions', and the hermeneutic type, in the form of 'interpretations of traditional complexes of meaning', are contrasted with two *critiques*: Marx's theory of society and Freud's metapsychology. Unlike the sciences, these critiques incorporate 'in their consciousness . . . an interest in emancipation going beyond the technical and the practical interest of knowledge'. Again, only in the critiques knowledge aims at self-reflection—that precious power relentlessly denied to science by Horkheimer's 'critical theory'.

For Habermas (1971, p. 9) there is a symmetry between the relation of theory to therapy in Freud and the relation of theory to praxis in Marxism. One is therefore tempted to conceive of his whole version of critical theory in terms of an equation: Praxis = reflexive therapy. What Habermas proposes constitutes the boldest fusion of Marx and Freud ever attempted since Marcuse's *Eros and Civilization* (1955).

Moreover, in striking contrast with Althusserian talmudic gospel-idolatry, Habermas is as willing as Marcuse to treat Marxism in all critical freedom, without trying to make up its tenets in order to adapt new realities (or newly recognized old ones) to the alleged 'completeness' of a pseudo-scientific dialectical materialism. Having no intellectually disastrous duties toward a political party thrown in chronic identity crises, the Frankfurt critical theorists easily avoid scholastic sophistry; theirs is a truly desacralized Marxism, and, at least in the case of Habermas, one intellectually much more demanding. Yet the question is: Does their Marxism, stripped of any doctrinaire fetishism, really tally with rational epistemological standards? Besides, does it even do real justice to what, in a truly scientific conception of social science, comes from Marx's views on social processes and social causation?

One of the essays in *Theory and Practice*, significantly entitled *Between Philosophy and Science: Marxism as Critique*, emphasizes the place of Marx on the top of a whole tradition in the philosophy of history. The Habermasian Marx, synthetizing Vico, Kant and Hegel, is, by the way, a superb reply to the Althusserian dehistorization of Marxism. In chapter 2 of *Knowledge and Human Interest*, however, Habermas addresses a severe reproach to Marx.

To understand why, let us follow his reasoning a little more closely.

Habermas's criticism of Marx rests on a distinction drawn between 'work' and 'interaction' (Habermas, 1971a, ch. 4). Both concepts are, as we have seen, antithetical Idealtypen adapted from Hegel's Jena *Phenomenology of Mind*: *work* is a social sphere virtually governed by self-evident *technical rules*; *interaction*, a social field governed by *social norms*, the observance of which always implies (unlike that of technical rules) some degree of dialogue and persuasion. Now Habermas praises Marx, the social historian, for the attention he paid to the interactive, communicative and self-reflective side of human striving; but he blames Marx, the philosopher and social theorist, for having neglected this very phenomenon, and having therefore conceived of human emancipation in terms of a process exclusively related to the realm of work and technical knowledge. Thus Marx is charged with a tendency—running from the writings of his youth up to the *Grundrisse*—to reduce the self-generating act of the human species to a naturalistic 'synthesis through social labour', oblivious of the specificity of the dialectics of interaction and symbolic communication.

Nor does the criticism stop here. In the main text of his second collection of essays, *Technik und Wissenschaft als 'Ideologie'* (1968), Habermas goes as far as to state that, in the analysis of advanced capitalism, the fundamental assumptions of historic materialism ought to be revised. According to him, the classic dualism of the forces of production and relations of production should be replaced by the more abstract antithesis between 'work' and 'interaction'. Likewise, since science has become itself a force of production, the economy has fallen under ample state regulations, and the class conflict has been impeded, a critical theory of society can no longer assume the form of a critique of political economy.

What are we to think of such an uninhibited theoretical revisionism? As the discussion of structural characteristics of present capitalist society is not within the scope of this chapter, we shall concentrate on the epistemologically relevant elements of Habermas's position. In this connection, I suggest we might begin by distinguishing his self-conscious problematic from his unspoken one. Habermas's avowed problematic in the early 1970s turns around the substantive and methodological difficulties pertaining to the concept of a reflexive socially emancipatory knowledge constructed on the basis of the psychoanalysis cathartic insight.

The first of such difficulties relates to the conceptual poverty of philosophy when it is summoned to clarify the *normative* aspect of analytic reflexion *as dialogue*. Starting from Fichte's notion of Mündigkeit, or mature autonomy, Habermas (1970) proceeds to outline a model of universal generative pragmatics capable of providing a 'code' for the concept of 'possible understanding'. Now though Habermas is anxious to acknowledge that his psychoanalytic paradigm needs 'disciplinary constraints' in order to avoid the ever-present danger of epistemological sloppiness, it may be found rather doubtful whether this unexpected, seeming 'Chomskyaniz-ation' of critical theory is a cognitive strategy good enough to satisfy the claims of scientific validity.

'The paradigm'—writes Habermas (1971a, p. 11)—'is no longer the observation but the dialogue.' And the dialogue he seems to think of is the vocationally *public* dialogue, the decline of which, after its promising beginnings in the Enlightenment, is deplored by Habermas since its first book, *Strukturwandel der Öffentlichkeit* (1962). One might say that for Habermas the Enlightenment ideal of philosophical debate has the same strong appeal as the classical ideal of the free citizen's political action has in Hannah Arendt's writings like *The Human Condition* (1958) or *Between Past and Future* (1959). Arendt's tradition-minded political theory ranks indeed among Habermas's chief theoretical inspirations, at least until *Theory and Practice*. Even her notion of a 'conquest' of the public 'sphere' and of public opinion by mass society (Arendt, 1958, ch. 6) heralds in a way Habermas's (1962, ch 5, 6) own obituary of independent public opinion in the structurally changed capitalist society of the welfare state and the mass media. But then one feels entitled to ask: Is not a Marxism as ready to dispense with the class-conflict perspective as Habermas's is dangerously close to the atomistic assumptions of 'mass society' pseudo-sociology, so rightly rejected by modern critical sociologies of communication (G. Cohn, 1973, ch. 4)?

As Habermas himself honestly admits (1971, pp. 15–16), one major problem in his epistemology is the difficulty of finding a suitable political translation for his therapeutic model of emancipatory dialogue—a point soon noticed by Oskar Negt (1971) in Germany and by John Rex (1974) in Britain. Habermas's reply to this objection consists in stressing the 'authority of the patient' by insisting on the repressive potential of organized enlightened praxis. Too much emphasis on the need for political organization, he warns, often ends by making us lose sight (as the young Lukács did) of the duty to preserve a living dialogue within that very institution—the radical party—originally created to translate emancipatory knowledge into concrete social action.

Thus, in 1971, denying himself the naïf Leninist illusions of infant Western Marxism, Habermas (who has for some years been a target of gauchiste activism in Germany) prefers to recede into an old soothing utopia of German progressism—the pedagogical solution: 'In the face of various sectarian enterprises, one might point out today that in advanced capitalism changing the structure of the general system of education might possibly be more important for the organization of enlightenment than the ineffectual training of cadres or the building of impotent parties' (ibid., pp. 31–32). In other words, if you can no longer trust the praxis of the radical left, then turn to the long-run promises of Bildung: join the classical Weimar club of pedagogical humanism . . . unless, of course, you suspect, as I do, that there is too much likeness between such a cultural utopianism and that persistent escape into the soul ominously bequeathed to the German mind by Lutheran a-political subjectivism.

So much for the avowed problematic of Habermas's theory. What about his unspoken one? Here, I believe, the heart of the matter is the problem of *culturalism*: the neo-idealistic obsession with a presumed duality of scientific knowledge, explicitly or implicitly derogatory of logico-empirical cognitive criteria. *Knowledge and Human Interest* criticizes Marx for his conceiving his own work as an intellectual effort substantially similar to natural science. To Habermas, Marxism is and ought to be a *critique*, not a science. The new introduction to *Theory and Practice* speaks of the 'chronic need for legitimation' which is developing today (the same theme overrides one of Habermas's latest books, the short *Legitimationsprobleme im Spätkapitalismus*, 1973); but the inside issue of *cognitive* legitimacy, that is, of proper standards and criteria of scientific truth, remains alien to the 'critial theorist's' preoccupations—or then is stubbornly overlooked as a simple positivistic query.

Once located 'between philosophy and science', neo-Marxian critique sets out to concentrate on superstructural phenomena (Habermas, 1971, p. 202); for Habermas, as he approves Claus Offe's (1969) contention about the emergence of 'political instrumentalities' relatively independent from the economic interests of capitalists in advanced capitalist society, greets the demise of the critique of political economy as the central weapon of critical social theory: 'Due to the introduction of elements of the superstructure into the base itself, the classical dependency relationship of politics to the economy was disrupted' (ibid., p. 237).

Thus culturalism tends to endorse one of the least perceptive among criticism of Marxian thought: that of economism. Here epistemological critical theory seems to share a current non sequitur: the arbitrary deduction of a 'meaninglessness' of economic causation from the mere recognition that the economy, and the interplay of polity and economy within society as a whole, have indeed changed with the evolution of capitalism. Besides, that economism is a misconstruction of Marx's social theory should not be easily forgotten. Marx was no economic reductionist; otherwise, *Capital* would never be written as a *critique* of political economy . . . after all, who did more than its author to *sociologize* (macro-) economic analysis? It was vulgar Marxism, rather than Marx, who disobeyed Max Weber's wise warning about the necessity of distinguishing between what is strictly economic, what is economically determined and what is only economically relevant.

As a social critic, Habermas does not match Adorno, the cultural critic. Adorno's global image of society suffers from soaring apocalyptical speculations, but his microsociological musical and literary critical essays highlight a host of major trends in Victorian and contemporary art; they count amongst the best landmarks in modern sociology of culture, whereas his pupil Habermas's achievement in substantive social analysis is up to now rather scanty. Nevertheless, the Habermasian vindication of enlightened reason *sub specie emancipationis*, in striking contrast to the older Frankfurtians's Kulturpessimismus, could, in principle, have increased the rate of rationality of modern Marx-inspired thinking. The pejorative but instructive nickname Lukács gave the Frankfurt school—'Grand Hotel Abyss'—no longer applies to critical theory since it turned to epistemology. It is therefore all the more unfortunate that the Habermasian rephrasing of critical theory remains so much under the spell of epistemologic irrationalism and of the anti-science bias. The pattern is typical: philosophy, we are told, ought to sit in judgment of positive science and its 'sins'; but the enquiry about the limits of science's validity is not at all to be conducted according to logico-empirical rules—rather, it is

performed under the inspiration of the holy ghost of a philosophy
of history . . . (for all the talk about critique's being placed midway
'between philosophy and science', the truth is that epistemological
critical theory is much more 'philosophical' than scientific; it
practically does not bother itself to knock down metaphysics and
reserves all the brunt of its attacks for 'positive science'
(Habermas, 1971, p. 238).

What is wrong with Habermasian critical theory is not so much
its 'philosophical' elements, often highly valuable (as when, in the
beginning of *Knowledge and Human Interest*, Kant is vindicated
against Hegel's scornful rejection of epistemologic scruples); it is
the *anthropomorphism* lurking beneath its proposed hierarchy of
types of knowledge. Emancipatory dialogical reflection remains a
humanistic ideal of knowledge, closer to wisdom than to real
'Galilean' knowledge. We gladly grant that emancipatory reflection is a nobly humane vision of knowledge, but the question is:
Does it faithfully depict the requirements of cognitive legitimacy?
If not, the epistemology of the Marxisant Dilthey, Jürgen
Habermas, is at bottom only slightly less gratuitous than the
phoney rival scholastic of the Marxist Comte, Louis Althusser.

(1975)

Notes

1 The veil and the mask: on ideology, power and legitimacy

1 Kluckhohn, 'Values and value-orientation in the theory of action', in Parsons and Shils (eds), *Toward a General Theory of Action*, part 4, ch. 2.

2 Smelser, *Theory of Collective Behaviour*, pp. 25–6 (emphasis added).

3 Cf. Durkheim, *The Elementary Forms of Religious Life*; Sapir, 'Symbolism', in *Selected Writings*, pp. 564–8; Lévi-Strauss, *Structural Anthropology*, ch. XI, and *Mythologies*; V. Turner, *The Forest of Symbols*. For a good survey of (lato sensu) sociological symbol theory, see Sir Raymond Firth's *Symbols: Public and Private*, chs 3–5; for a provocative critical revision of this heritage, see D. Sperber, *Rethinking Symbolism*.

4 Seliger, *Ideology and Politics*, p. 120 (emphasis added).

5 Lukes, *Emile Durkheim*, p. 440.

6 See Barbu, *Society, Culture and Personality*, pp. 103–7.

7 For the claim that ideology cannot but be partial, see Plamenatz, *Ideology*, pp. 17–18.

8 For a criticism of Mannheim's reduction of ideology to élite cultural production, see Peter Hamilton, *Knowledge and Social Structure*, p. 132.

9 Giddens, *Capitalism and Modern Social Theory*, p. 213.

10 See the concluding chapter of Landes's masterful analysis of nineteenth-century European technological change and industrialization, in *The Unbound Prometheus*.

11 I cannot therefore agree with Gabel (*Idéologies*, p. 26), who defines ideology as a 'theoretical crystallization' of false consciousness. As for the expression 'secular scripture', I borrow it from N. Frye's homonymous book.

12 R. E. Lane, *Political Ideology*.

13 This theoretical dichotomy has been forcefully established by Geertz,

'Ideology as a cultural system' (now ch. 8 of *The Interpretation of Cultures*); it has been recently revived by Carlton, *Ideology and Social Order*, ch. 3.

14 For the refutation of an instinctivist reading of Pareto, see Finer, in the introductions to his edition of Vilfredo Pareto, *Sociological Writings*, pp. 42–3. While valuing (p. 82) the role of Pareto's work in the dismissal of unicausal models of social change, Professor Finer asserts (p. 78) that Pareto could have developed a supplementation of marxist analysis but did in fact try to replace the latter with a psychological theory blind to the social composition of élites and to its bearing on any satisfactory account of processes of élite circulation. Finer's introduction also highlights (pp. 73, 77) the circularity of residue theory: Pareto infers residues from their manifestations, yet assumes they are the cause of the latter.

15 This criticism of Scheler is actually made by Merton, *Social Theory and Social Structure*, p. 535.

16 The expression comes from Geertz, *The Interpretation of Cultures*, p. 203.

17 Theorists like Lévi-Strauss conceive of myth and art as major providers of these 'imaginary mediations' for the contradictions of society; see his 'Introduction à l'oeuvre de Marcel Mauss', in Mauss, *Sociologie et Anthropologie*, pp. XIX–XX (commented upon in Merquior, *L'Esthétique de Lévi-Strauss*, ch. 1).

18 Geertz, op. cit., points out this Freudo-Durkheimian element as essential to the Parsonian strain theory of ideology.

19 Birnbaum, 'The sociological analysis of ideology (1940–60)', reprinted as ch. 1 of *Toward a Critical Sociology*, p. 55.

20 Hamilton, op. cit., p. 29.

21 Vincent, *Fétichisme et société*, p. 223.

22 Cf. Lapassade and Lourau, *Clefs pour la sociologie*, p. 101.

23 Popper, *The Open Society and its Enemies*, ch. II, pp. 94–6.

24 Merton's warning against the facile endorsement of debunking interest theories resting (often unawares) on the Hobbesian idea of egoism as the motive force of conduct (*Social Theory and Social Structure*, p. 554) is a case in point.

25 Stark, *The Sociology of Knowledge*, p. 100.

26 Althusser, 'Idéologie et Appareils Idéologiques d'Etat', in La Pensée no. 151 (June 1970), pp. 3–38. English translation in *Lenin and Philosophy and Other Essays*.

27 Lukes's book provides a fair critical synthesis of Dahl's theory, and of that of his American critics.

28 Lukes, *Power: A Radical View*, p. 21.

29 Op cit., pp. 23–5.

30 Cf. Bradshaw, 'A critique of Steven Lukes's *Power: A Radical View*, in *Sociology*, vol. 10, no. 1 (January 1976), p. 121.

31 Wrong, 'Problems in defining power', now ch. 10 of his *Skeptical Sociology*.

32 Wrong, *Skeptical Sociology*, p. 165.

33 Lukes, op. cit., p. 24.

34 Ibid. (footnote).
35 Lukes, 'Reply to Bradshaw', in *Sociology*, vol. 10, no. 1 (January 1976), p. 130.
36 Lukes, *Power*, p. 33.
37 A. Cohen, *Two-Dimensional Man: An Essay on the Anthropology of Power and Symbolism in Complex Society*, p. 10.
38 On this particular point see Firth, *Elements of Social Organization*.
39 In fact, there is no need to take it at such a level; although his book is committed to the demonstration that there is no such thing as culture as an independent system, but only a collection of norms, values and beliefs structured in social situations, clearly its main thrust (apart from the provocative discussion of the telos of anthropology) consists much more in mapping out a cluster of symbolic strategies connected with kinds of groups than in giving any elaborate explanation of these connections; in this sense, and despite its wish to avoid merely descriptive anthropology by insisting on the analysis of the relations between the major variables of symbolic action and power relationships (p. 10), Cohen's volume is of an heuristic, rather than explanatory, character.
40 R. Martin, *The Sociology of Power*, especially chs. 3, 4 and 11. Martin draws chiefly on Buckley and Etzioni for some of his central concepts, but arrives at an original and, to my mind, more comprehensive view of power, supplemented by an illuminating macrosociological typology of patterns of domination resting on different systems of labour exploitation.
41 The accusation seems to me quite unjust, at least if meant literally. Weber's famous definition of power (*Economy and Society*, vol. I, p. 53) as 'the probability that one actor in a social relationship will . . . carry out his own will' clearly denotes the *relational* aspect rather than an individual attribute, since the assessment of the probability of the exercise of power is up to the virtual power subject. After all, the definition presupposes Weber's concept of social action, with all its *verstehende* overtones. Naturally, as Wrong (op. cit., p. 171) remarks, one should avoid falling into an extreme *reputational* theory of power (otherwise beliefs about power would never be illusory); but this only restores the balance within the relational nature of power ('powers are relations, not things', wrote Locke). On the other hand, one can, of course, avoid defining power as the attribute of an individual and nevertheless drop the Weberian sense of the coercive; this is just what Hannah Arendt does in her *On Violence*, pp. 40–52, where power, as distinct from violence, is defined as an always legitimate, consensual *potestas in populo*, and explicitly dissociated from the 'business of dominion'.
42 Cf. Parsons, 'On the concept of political power', now in Parsons, *Politics and Social Structure*, pp. 352–404.
43 Giddens, 'Power in the recent writings of Talcott Parsons', in *Sociology*, vol. 2, 1968.
44 Martin, op. cit., pp. 50, 55.
45 Op. cit., pp. 41–2.

46 Bachrach and Baratz, op. cit., ch. 2.
47 The authors actually speak of power both as a general concept and as synonymous with coercion. We follow a suggestion made by Lukes (op. cit., p. 17) and reserve the noun power for the general concept.
48 For Easton, see his essay 'The perception of authority and political change' in C. J. Friedrich (ed.), *Authority*, in Nomos I; for Simmel, see the introduction to the second part of his *Soziologie* (trans. in *The Sociology of Georg Simmel*, ed. by K. Wolff, pp. 181–3).
49 Bachrach and Baratz, op. cit., p. 28.
50 Martin, op. cit., p. 56.
51 Blau, *Exchange and Power in Social Life*, pp. 205–13; Wrong, *Skeptical Sociology*, pp. 188, 195.
52 de Jouvenel, 'Authority: the efficient imperative', in Carl J. Friedrich (ed.), *Authority*, Nomos I.
53 Stinchcombe, *Constructing Social Theories*, pp. 162–3.
54 Op. cit., p. 183.
55 Op. cit., pp. 108–9. Selznick's work on which Stinchcombe draws is *Leadership in Administration*.
56 Perkin, *The Origin of Modern British Society*, pp. 219–20.
57 Parkin, *Class Inequality and Political Order*, p. 93. The whole of chapter 3 deals with the problem of 'class inequality and meaning systems'.
58 Martin, op. cit., p. 165. See especially Mueller, *The Politics of Communication: A Study in the Political Sociology of Language, Socialization and Legitimation*. Bernstein's best known book is *Class, Codes and Control*, of which, in this connection, chs. 3, 6 and 9 are of particular importance.
59 Wallerstein, *The Modern World System*, p. 143.
60 Ibid., p. 144.
61 For a critical discussion of Gramsci's central concept, hegemony, see P. Anderson, 'The Antinomies of Gramsci', *New Left Review*, no. 100 (1976).
62 Gellner, 'Concepts and Society', now ch. 2 of *Cause and Meaning in the Social Sciences*.
63 Cf. Gellner, 'Is belief really necessary?', now ch. 5 of *The Devil in Modern Philosophy*.
64 *The Devil in Modern Philosophy*, pp. 59–60.
65 This is a point well developed in ch. 8 of Gellner's *Thought and Change*. For a nostalgic opposite view, deploring the cultural effects of the 'retreat from the world' after the 'classic literacy' era and the 'age of the book', see G. Steiner's books *Language and Silence* and *Extraterritorial*.
66 Topitsch, *Vom Ursprung und Ende der Metaphysik—eine Studie zur Weltanschauungskritik*, and also his 'Max Weber and Sociology Today' in the homonymous book edited by Stammer, pp. 21–2.
67 'Criticalist', because the philosopher chiefly responsible for the demotion of belief is Popper, whose *logic* of scientific discovery (contrariwise to Michael Polanyi's or Thomas Kuhn's explorations into the *psychology* of science) has no decisive room for fideistic belief.

68 See Gouldner, *The Dialectic of Ideology and Technology*.
69 Polanyi, *The Great Transformation*, p. 152 (but see also p. 184).
70 Gouldner, 'Reciprocity and autonomy in functional theory', now ch. 7 of *For Sociology*.
71 This paradox has just been suggestively highlighted by Albert Hirschman in Part Three of his *The Passions and the Interests: Political Arguments for Capitalism Before its Triumph*.
72 For the Paretian affinities of Lenin's concept of ideology, see Plamenatz, op. cit., pp. 140–1.
73 For a good critical assessment of Sorel, see S. P. Rouanet, 'Irrationalism and Myth in Georges Sorel', *The Review of Politics*, University of Notre Dame Press, January 1964.
74 Feuer, *Ideology and the Ideologists*; Shils, 'The concept and function of ideology', *International Encyclopaedia of the Social Sciences*, vol. 7, pp. 66–75.
75 Commenting on this historical paradox, Wallerstein (op. cit., p. 62) warns against the vacuousness of holding any 'primacy of values' in social causation. But, after chiding the tenants of such a primacy for assuming far more literal a correspondence between thought forms and social basis than ever did Marxism, he also states (*ibid.*) that the different historical roles of individualism in the West and in Ming China are a proof of the causal weakness of ideology. This last statement, however, is a quite sweeping one, and as such rather out of tune in a study as serious—and rewarding—and as bold as *The Modern System* is. For the assertion of a general causal weakness of ideology generalizes from the assumption that the individualism of the Ming mandarins and that of Western erstwhile capitalist entrepreneurs is the same ideology—an assumption which does not hold, since, as we have just argued, sociological analysis, by relating these two individualisms to their respective social bases, and to the function of the latter in distinct historical processes, shows that they are only superficially the same (in other words, their surface *intellectual* meaning may be common, but their deep *social* function differed decisively). Wallerstein's mistake is basically analogous with Lucien Goldmann's much debated contention that a *few* world-views have been successively held by *many* different social classes throughout history. In the Brussels colloquium on sociology of literature and psychoanalysis, the late Roger Bastide claimed that such a thesis is anything but Marxist, since it clearly violates the principle of rooting ideology on historically specific—and therefore, hardly repeatable—class positions. We do not have to bother about Goldmann's being faithful or not to his professed Marxism to recognize that Bastide was right as to the gist of the matter: as far as their social functions are concerned, ideologies could not possibly be 'few' if their social bases were not. If the meaning of ideology before its being sociologically explained and its meaning after such an explanation could coincide, the sociology of ideology would simply lose its raison d'être. But if it does not, then it becomes impossible to assert the 'sameness' of ideologies irrespective of their social bases.

76 See, for instance, L. B. Brown, *Ideology*, p. 172—a sensible psychological approach, focusing on individual behaviour and not on ideologies as systems of ideas.
77 Brown, op. cit., p. 177. Cf. also Hudson, *Frames of Mind*.
78 Geertz, *The Interpretation of Cultures*, p. 207.
79 Bourdieu, *Outline of a Theory of Practice*, p. 164.
80 Ibid.
81 Bourdieu, op. cit., p. 86.

2 Remarks on the theory of culture

1 Kroeber and Kluckhohn, *Culture: A Critical Review of Concepts and Definitions*.
2 Cf. Cicero, *Tusc. Disp.*, 1, 13 (cultura animi philosophia est). The suggestion that the Latin *cultura* in this humanistic sense translated the Greek *paideia* was made by Werner Jaeger, quoted in Arendt, *Between Past and Future*, ch. VI, n. 6; as to the Ciceronian second translation of *paideia* as *humanitas*, see Marrou, *Saint Augustin et la fin de la culture antique*, pp. 552–4, and Pfeiffer, *History of Classical Scholarship 1300–1850*, p. 15. For a brief recall of the crystallization of the *cultura animi* ideal from Plutarch to modern classicism, see Bauman, *Culture as Praxis*, pp. 7–8. Bauman aptly presents Aristotle's likening of the soul to 'the capacity of a tool' (*De Anima*, II, i, 1) and in general the Aristotelian analogy between soul-perfection and *techne* as the natural philosophical basis of the Ciceronian-Plutarchan perfective view of culture. On the creative reprise of the humanistic ideal by the Weimarian quest for an expressive yet perfective self, on the threshold of the Industrial Revolution, see the classic 1909 study by Spranger, *Wilhelm von Humboldt und die Humanitätsidee*.
3 Cochrane, *Christianity and Classical Culture*; Curtius, *European Literature and the Latin Middle Ages*; Highet, *The Classical Tradition—Greek and Roman Influences on Western Literature*; Bolgar, *The Classical Heritage and its Beneficiaries*; Jaeger, *Early Christianity and Greek Paideia*.
4 The standard history of historicism is still Meinecke's *Die Entstehung des Historismus*, which embraces the period comprehended between Hamann and Ranke, giving a central place to Hamann's great disciple, Herder. See also Niedermann, *Kultur—Werden und Wandlungen des Begriffes und seiner Ersatzsbegriffe von Cicero bis Herder*. 'Historicism' is a tricky concept. Actually, one could attach not just two, but at least four meanings to it. (a) In the sence relevant to Herder, historicism means a stress on historical individuality and indeed uniqueness, and as such was the subject of Meinecke's study. Its models are Herder, Burke and romantic or late romantic jurists, historians and philologists, from Savigny and Ranke (Meinecke's hero) to Droysen—not Hegelian or Marxist philosophy of history. (b) In Anglo-Saxon usage, on the other hand, as we saw, Hegel and Marx were until lately precisely what was chiefly connoted by 'historicism', since Popper's influential onslaught on historical prediction. In addition, there are two

other meanings, both, like Popper's, outright pejorative: (c) one, the eldest of this highly equivocal semantical family, dates back from the economist Carl Menger's *Die Irrthümer des Historismus* (1884). Menger bestowed the label upon the younger branch of the so-called 'historical school' in German economics, whose leader was Gustav Schmoller. As Hayek (*The Counter-Revolution of Science*, p. 215) recalls, the conceptual chasm between Historismus in the original Mengerian sense, and Meinecke's homonym, may be easily inferred from the fact that the marginalist thought of Menger, stressing as it did 'organic' institutions (i.e., those which, like the market, are not artifacts, not products of deliberate creation), got accused by Schmoller of adhering to Burke and Savigny's organicist social philosophy! To that extent Menger, the coiner of 'Historismus' in sense (c), would feature as a historist himself in sense (a). Finally, (d), for Althusser and his followers, 'historicism' is the very reverse of Marxist structuralism: an idealist distortion closely akin to 'humanism'; historicism is for them the inability to perform history as structural science, as well as the tendency to substitute monolithic 'totalities' for genuine structural processes. From this viewpoint, *both* Hegelianism, the theory of unfolding Totality, *and* the mystique of historical uniqueness are forms of the historicist sin. In other words, historicism in our sense (d) lumps (a) and (b) together in detestation.

5 Elias, *Über den Prozess der Zivilisation*, I, ch. 1.
6 See Isaiah Berlin, Vico and Herder, especially pp. 195–9.
7 See Mauss, 'Les Civilisations: éléments et formes' (in Mauss et al., *Civilisation: le mot et l'idée*) and Alfred Weber, *Prinzipien der Geschichte—und Kulturgeschichte als Kultursoziologie*, appendix, section III. A. Weber's dichotomy strongly recalls Spengler's famous opposition between the 'spiritual' culture of Greece and the 'material' civilization of Rome. See also Thomas Mann, *Betrachtungen eines Unpolitischen*.
8 Cf. Manuel, *Shapes of Philosophical History*, p. 77.
9 Bauman, op. cit., ch. 1.
10 Ibid., pp. 18–19. On the other hand, Raymond Williams has just acknowledged Herder as the first author to use 'the significant plural, *cultures*, in distinction from a singular . . . unilinear sense of *civilization*' (cf. his 'Developments in the sociology of culture', in *Sociology* vol. 10, no. 3 (1976), p. 497).
11 Ibid., p. 26.
12 Berlin, op. cit., pp. XXII–XXIII, 199.
13 Barbu, *Society, Culture and Personality*, pp. 78–81.
14 Tylor, *Primitive Culture*, vol. I, pp. 1–3 (emphasis added).
15 Ibid.
16 The recognition that Tylor and the other Victorian evlutionists were not interested in concrete culture areas, but in culture as a general overall process, and thereby did not as much 'legislate' to each and one culture as to mankind as a whole, seen from a broad macrohistorical standpoint, was part of the reaction against the 'anti-evolutionist fallacy' (see the now classic 1945 Leslie White article in *American*

Anthropologist, 47; see also Nisbet, *Social Change and History*, pp. 224–5). Tylor also kept off the proto-structuralism (in Radcliffe-Brown's sense) of Maine and McLennan. Unlike them, he did not cultivate (however speculatively) institutional analysis. His treatment of religion was psychological, not sociological. Unconcerned with cultural Gestalten, he contented himself to rescue primitive religion from Max Müller's derogatory remarks about myth as the pathology of language, without bothering—any more than Frazer—to draw armchair connections between belief and the rest of tribal customs. For these important differences among classic anthropologists, see Burrow, *Evolution and Society: A Study in Victorian Social Theory*, pp. 237–9. However, I. M. Lewis (*Social Anthropology in Perspective*, ch. 2) has just detected functionalist tendencies in Tylor. In his path-breaking application of statistics to social sciences, more specifically, in his pursuing valid correlations, between avoidance behaviour and the marriage-residence regime in primitive societies, Tylor the evolutionist becomes indeed a true forerunner of the healthiest aspects of functionalist method.

17 Kroeber, *Anthropology*, section 112.
18 Ibid., section 113
19 Ibid., section 132.
20 Ibid., section 117–19.
21 Leslie White, *The Evolution of Culture*; see Kotta, 'Histoire de la pensée ethnologique', in Poirier (ed.), *Ethnologie générale*, p. 82.
22 See Bidney, *Theoretical Anthropology*; but Bidney's rickety epistemology has in turn been laid bare by D. Kaplan in 'The Superorganic: science or metaphysics?' (in Manners and Kaplan, op. cit., pp. 20–31).
23 Geertz, *The Interpretation of Cultures*, ch. 3.
24 Moscovici, *La Société contre nature*, p. 108.
25 Popper, 'Of clouds and clocks' (now ch. 6 of *Objective Knowledge*, where chs 3, 4 and 8 are also of related interest). 'World 3' corresponds to Frege's 'third realm'.
26 Popper, *Unended Quest*, section 38–9.
27 Medawar, *The Uniqueness of the Individual*. Popper, *Unended Quest*, section 38–9.
28 Bauman, op. cit., p. 115.
29 Kroeber, op. cit., section 122 (integration) and 125 (ethos/eidos and values).
30 For Kroeber's appreciation of Benedict, see his *Anthropology*, op. cit., section 135; we find a more lucid appraisal in Bastide, *Sociologie et psychanalyse*, ch. VII. For his historicist epistemology, see Kroeber, 'History and science in anthropology'—a 1935 paper that converted the best British anthropologist, Evans-Pritchard, formerly a naturalist in epistemology like his master Radcliffe-Brown, into an influential historicist (see Evans-Pritchard, *Social Anthropology*, pp. 60–1).
31 Steward, 'Levels of sociocultural integration: an operational concept', in Manners and Kaplan (eds), *Theory in Anthropology*, p. 127.
32 Kroeber, op. cit., section 126.

33 Linton, *The Study of Man*.
34 Wissler, *Man and Culture*.
35 *Encyclopaedia of the Social Sciences* (1931), vol. IV, pp. 621–46. For a review of Malinowski's views on culture before his late attempt to systematization in *A Scientific Theory of Culture*, see Audrey Richards, 'The concept of culture in Malinowski's work', in Firth (ed.), *Man and Culture*, pp. 15–31.
36 Malinowski, *A Scientific Theory of Culture*, p. 125.
37 For Parsons's own standard presentation of this model (worked out in the early 1950s with Bales and Shils), see his *Societies: Evolutionary and Comparative Perspectives*, ch. 2.
38 Steward, op. cit., pp. 127–30.
39 Lévi-Strauss, 'Introduction à l'oeuvre de Marcel Mauss', in Mauss, *Sociologie et anthropologie*, p. XIX.
40 Lévi-Strauss, *Structural Anthropology*, ch. XV, section 4, a.
41 See Kaplan and Manners, *Culture Theory*, p. 193.
42 Sperber, 'Contre certains a priori anthropologiques', in Morin et al., *L'Unité de l'homme*, pp. 491–4; Geertz, 'The impact of the concept of culture on the concept of man', ch. 2 of *The Interpretation of Cultures*, op. cit., pp. 43–51.
43 Sperber, op. cit., pp. 495–6.
44 Geertz, op. cit., p. 45.
45 Ibid., p. 44.
46 Blumer, 'Sociological implications of the thought of George Herbert Mead', *AJS*, March 1966, reprinted in Wallace (ed.), *Sociological Theory*, pp. 234–44.
47 Parsons, 'The superego and the theory of social systems', in Parsons, Bales and Shils, *Working Papers in the Theory of Action*.
48 Parsons, *The Social System*, p. 44.
49 Wrong, 'The oversocialized conception of man in modern sociology', in *ASR*, XXVI; reprinted as ch. 2 of Wrong, *Skeptical Sociology*.
50 Dahrendorf, 'Homo Sociologicus', now in *Essays in the Theory of Society*, ch. 2.
51 Rocher, *Talcott Parsons et la sociologie américaine*, p. 231.
52 Dawe, 'The Two Sociologies', *British Journal of Sociology*, vol. 21, reprinted in Thompson and Tunstall (eds), *Sociological Perspectives*, pp. 542–54.
53 Parsons, *The Social System*, p. 42.
54 Ibid, p. 36.
55 Bocock, *Freud and Modern Society*, p. 52.
56 For the Hobbesian approach of Malinowski's view of man, see I. M. Lewis, op. cit., p. 53.
57 For a good account of this new theoretical look in British anthropology, see Kuper, *Anthropologists and Anthropology: the British School 1922–72*, pp. 160–6.
58 Nadel, *The Theory of Social Structure*, pp. 52–5.
59 Goffman, *Stigma: Notes on the Management of Spoiled Identity*.
60 Simmel, *Grundfragen der Soziologie (Individuum und Gesellschaft)*,

ch. IV, translated in Wolff (ed.), *The Sociology of Georg Simmel*, pp. 58–84.

61 Parsons, *The Structure of Social Action*, chs 8–12.

62 See the translation of his 1914 essay, 'Le dualisme de la nature humaine et ses conditions sociales', in K. H. Wolff (ed.), *Emile Durkheim, 1858–1917: A Collection of Essays*, pp. 325–40.

63 Bauman, *Towards a Critical Sociology*, p. 23.

64 I take it that such an interpretation of Freud is by now the standard one. For an authoritative exposition, see Rieff, *Freud: The Mind of the Moralist*, passim, and especially ch. 10.

65 Bastide, *Sociologie et psychanalyse*, p. 285.

66 Foucault, *The Order of Things*, ch. 10, section V.

67 Róheim, *The Origin and Function of Culture*, part III.

68 Martindale, *Sociological Theory and the Problem of Values*, p. 68.

69 The formula 'metaphysical research programmes', in the sense of nonfalsifiable (hence non-scientific) yet rationally criticizable theories, is Sir Karl Popper's. The term is the subject of his unpublished *Postscript* to the *Logic of Scientific Discovery*, according to *Unended Quest*, n. 242, as well as of sections 33 and 37 of the latter book, where a metaphysical research programme such as Darwinism is said to be 'a possible framework for testable scientific theories'; the main idea occurs also in *Conjectures and Refutations*, ch. 8, part 2. Popper has always labelled psychoanalysis a 'pseudoscientific theory' (*Unended Quest*, section 9), though he has passingly recognized that much of what Freud stated 'may well play its part one day in a psychological science which is testable' (*Conjectures and Refutations*, p. 37). But an outstanding psychologist like Bruner ('The Freudian conception of man and the continuity of nature', in *Daedalus*, no. 87, reprinted in Brodbeck (ed.), *Readings in the Philosophy of the Social Sciences*, op. cit., pp. 705–11) has claimed that Freud's mode of thought, not being a theory in the conventional scientific sense, 'is the ground from which theory will grow'. In other words: it will very likely increasingly qualify as a 'framework for testable theories'. Barbu (op. cit., p. 164), writing from the standpoint of social psychology, sums up the matter as he warns against any deducing from all-inclusive concepts of personality like the Freudian a whole range of institutions, cultural systems and historical processes, while recognizing that psychoanalysis supplied social science with useful general ideas and even working hypotheses.

70 Rieff, 'Towards a theory of culture' in Nossiter (ed.), *Imagination and Precision in the Social Sciences*, p. 99.

71 Riesman et al., *The Lonely Crowd*, ch. I, 1.

72 Kluckhohn, 'Values and value orientations', in Parsons and Shils (eds), *Toward a General Theory of Action*, p. 399.

3 Methodological infrastructuralism: an approach to the sociology of culture

1 Thus Martindale, *Sociological Theory and the Problem of Values*,

p. VIII: 'The sociology of the 1970s might be characterized by the attempt to bring coherence to the sociology of culture.'

2 MacRae, 'Introduction' to Percy S. Cohen, *Modern Social Theory*, p. VIII.

3 Robertson, 'Toward the identification of the major axes of sociological analysis', in Rex (ed.), *Approaches to Sociology*, pp. 111, 113, 119.

4 Radcliffe-Brown, *A Natural Science of Society*, p. 106—a warning which is clearly an objection to Malinowski.

5 Sorokin, *Socio-cultural Causality, Space and Time*.

6 For a sharp denunciation of this culturalist bias in Parsons's neo-evolutionism, see Anthony D. Smith, *The Concept of Social Change*, op. cit., pp. 37–42. As Smith points out, such a culturalist 'cybernetic' model eventually destroys Parsons's intentions as to achieving a systemic analysis.

7 Radcliffe-Brown, op. cit., p. 106.

8 Blake and Davis, 'On norms and values', in Manners and Kaplan (eds), *Theory in Anthropology*, op. cit., pp. 465–72.

9 Aberle, 'The influence of linguistics on early culture and personality theory', in Manners and Kaplan (eds), op. cit., p. 315.

10 Blake and Davis, op. cit.

11 See the first footnote to part III of Mannheim, *Essays on the Sociology of Culture*.

12 Included in Mannheim, *Essays on Sociology and Social Psychology* (ch. 2).

13 These differences between the *Ideology and Utopia* period and the sociology of culture essays, the last Mannheim wrote before leaving Germany, are stressed by Ernest Mannheim in his introduction to the British edition (see n. 11 above).

14 Part II in *Essays on the Sociology of Culture*.

15 Geertz, *The Interpretation of Cultures*, op. cit., p. 14 (emphasis added).

16 Steward, *Theory of Culture Change*.

17 Nimkoff and Middleton, 'Types of family and types of economy', in Yehudi Cohen (ed.), *Man in Adaptation: The Cultural Present*, pp. 384–93.

18 Harris, *The Rise of Anthropological Theory*, p. 662.

19 As is wisely acknowledged by Kaplan and Manners, op. cit., p. 121.

20 Gouldner and Peterson, *Notes on Technology and the Moral Order*.

21 Y. Cohen, 'Adaptation and evolution', in Y. Cohen (ed.), *Man in Adaptation: The Institutional Framework*.

22 Gellner, *Legitimation of Belief*, p. 86.

23 Gellner, *Cause and Meaning in the Social Sciences*, p. 124.

24 Cf. Lévi-Strauss, *The Savage Mind*, ch. IX.

25 Nagel, *Logic without Metaphysics*; see also his illuminating 1954 address, 'Naturalism reconsidered', reprinted in P. Kurtz (ed.), *American Philosophy in the Twentieth Century*, pp. 544–55.

26 Cf. Gellner, 'Sociology and social anthropology', now in *Cause and Meaning in the Social Sciences*, pp. 107–37.

27 Gellner, *Legitimation of Belief*, pp. 98–107.

28 Piaget, *Etudes sociologiques*, ch. 1.
29 Aron, 'Marxisme critique ou dogmatique', in *Playdoyer pour une Europe décadente*, p. 120.
30 Marx and Engels, *The German Ideology*, p. 47
31 Jakubowski, *Ideology and Superstructure*, ch. 2.
32 Ibid.
33 Brinkman, 'Der "Überbau" und die Wissenschaften von Staat und Gesellschaft', reprinted in *Wirtschaftsformen und Lebensformen*.
34 Scheler, *Die Wissensformen und die Gesellschaft*.
35 Merton, *Social Theory and Social Structure*, p. 533.
36 Worsley, 'The kinship system of the Tallensi: a revaluation', *Journal of the Royal Anthropological Institute*, no. 86 (1956); Fortes, *Kinship and the Social Order*, pp. 220ff.
37 Sahlins, *Culture and Practical Reason*, p. 6.
38 Gluckman, 'Social beliefs and individual thinking in tribal society', in Manners and Kaplan (eds), *Theory in Anthropology*, pp. 462–5.
39 Cobban, *Aspects of the French Revolution*, ch. 5.
40 This is well acknowledged by a leading Marxist historian like Hobsbawm; see his *Age of Revolution*, ch. 10.
41 Geertz, op. cit., pp. 143–4. Geertz's position is quoted with approval by Sztompka, *System and Function*, p. 160.
42 Rieff, 'Towards a theory of culture', op. cit., p. 106.
43 Chaunu, *Le Temps des réformes: la crise de la chrétienté 1250–1550*, pp. 12–30 and passim.
44 Classically emphasized by Troeltsch, *The Social Teaching of the Christian Churches,* vol. 1.
45 Lucien Febvre and Henri-Jean Martin, *The Coming of the Book: The Impact of Printing, 1450–1800*.
46 Hempel, *Aspects of Scientific Explanation*.

4 Psychology in its place

1 Hayek, *The Counter-Revolution of Science*, ch. IV. The expression 'methodological individualism', though it occurs in Hayek's text (originally dating back to 1942) seems to have been consecrated by Popper (*Open Society*, vol. II, p. 91). But Weber himself—the patron saint of the idea—had already written that 'sociology . . . must adopt strictly *individualistic methods*' (quoted by Mommsen, 'Max Weber's Political Sociology and his Philosophy of World History', *International Social Science Journal*, XVII (1965), p. 25; emphasis added). However, as Lukes (Individualism, p. 111) correctly observes, Weber was far from following his own rule, even in his account of the 'rationalization' of culture.
2 Jarvie, *Concepts and Society*, op. cit., appendix.
3 Agassi, 'Methodological individualism', *British Journal of Sociology*, vol. 11.
4 Gellner, 'Explanation in history', reprinted as ch. 1 of *Cause and Meaning in the Social Sciences*.
5 Lukes, *Individualism*, op cit., pp. 117–21.

6 P. Cohen, *Modern Social Theory, op. cit.*, p. 94.
7 Piaget, *Introduction à l'épistémologie génétique*, vol. 3, pp. 193–4.
8 A strongly antipsychologistic use of the 'action frame of reference' is also preferred by Rex, *Key Problems of Sociological Theory*, ch. V.
9 The argument is White's, *The Evolution of Culture*, pp. 13–14.
10 On this point, see Kaplan and Manners, op. cit., pp. 135–7.
11 Inkeles, 'Personality and social structure', in Merton et al. (eds), *Sociology Today*, pp. 249–76.
12 Runciman, *Sociology in its Place*, pp. 7, 10, 39.
13 Freud, *New Introductory Lectures*, Standard Edition, vol. XXII, p. 179.
14 Runciman, op cit., p. 41.
15 Barbu, *Society, Culture and Personality*, op. cit., p. 173.
16 Gay, *Art and Act: On Causes in History*, p. 27.
17 Ekeh, *Social Exchange Theory*, p. 97.

5 The symbolic; or culture, value and symbol

1 Kroeber and Parsons, 'The concepts of culture and social system', *ASR*, 23.
2 White, *The Science of Culture; A Study of Man and Civilization*, p. 29.
3 Bauman, *Culture as Praxis*, p. 51.
4 Martinet, *Eléments de linguistique générale*, ch. 1. For a masterful discussion of the similarities and differences between animal symbolic communication and human language, see Benveniste, 'Communication animale et langage humain', *Diogène*, no. 1 (1952), reprinted as ch. 5 of his *Problèmes de linguistique générale*; also Mounin, 'Communication linguistique humaine et communication non-linguistique animale', in *Introduction à la sémiologie*, pp. 41–56. On double articulation, see also Lepschy, *La Linguistica Strutturale*, p. 133.
5 'Explanatory attitudes' is Barbu's (*Society, Culture and Personality*, p. 96) formula; 'reflective choice' comes from Hartung, 'Behaviour, culture and symbolism', in Dole and Carneiro (eds), *Essays in the Science of Culture in Honor of Leslie A. White*, p. 233. Behaviourist *non*-symbolic theory of normative conduct, as stated by Finley Scott in *Internalization of Norms: a Sociological Theory of Moral Commitment*, tends to neglect these important differences between man and animal, which are not in the least incompatible with the existence of infra-human forms of symbol communication. For a good criticism of F. Scott's position, see Ekeh, *Social Exchange Theory*, pp. 103–10.
6 Benveniste, *Problèmes*, op. cit., pp. 60–2.
7 Leroi-Gourhan, *Le Geste et la parole*, vol II, ch. 1, pp. 17–22.
8 Geertz, op. cit., ch. 1, especially pp. 5, 49 (symbols as prerequisites of culture).
9 Kluckhohn et al., 'Values and value-orientations in the theory of action', in Parsons and Shils (eds), *Toward a General Theory of Action*, part 4, ch. 2.
10 Ibid., pp. 413–19.
11 Ibid., pp. 423–32.

12 Smelser, op. cit., pp. 25–6 (emphasis added).
13 See Frye, *The Secular Scripture*, where this expression applies to narrative culture with its two main groups of stories, the *mythical* (stories built upon central social values) and the *fabulous* (stories built upon peripheral values).
14 Lazarsfeld, 'A typology of disposition concepts', *AJS*, vol. 65, no 1 (1959), reprinted as ch. 11 of *Qualitative Analysis*, op. cit.
15 Lévi-Strauss, 'Introduction à l'oeuvre de M. Mauss', op. cit., pp. XLVII–XLIX.
16 Firth, *Symbols: Public and Private*, chs 3–5.
17 Gadamer, *Truth and Method*, pp. 65–7.
18 Firth, op. cit., p. 144.
19 Sapir, 'Symbolism', *Encyclopaedia of the Social Sciences*, vol. XIV; reprinted in *Selected Writings*, pp. 564–8.
20 See Burke, *The Philosophy of Literary Form*; Frye, *Anatomy of Criticism*; Bachelard, *La Poétique de l'espace*; Barthes (who is occasionally also a trans-literary semiologist, as we can see from his *Mythologies* and especially his *Système de la mode*), *Essais critiques* and *S/Z* (we exclude on purpose criticism deriving in an orthodox way from the various psychoanalytical sects). For Geertz's reference (which actually names only Burke) see his *Interpretation of Cultures*, op. cit., pp. 29, 92. It is a pity Firth's chapters on the history of symbol theory, though ready to draw on some literary criticism focusing on the poetic-symbol tradition, romantic (Feidelson) or symbolist (Michaud), do not show any acquaintance with these, and several other, much more illuminating critics. By contrast, the forceful but too schematic interpretation of romanticism as a style of the symbol advocated by Wellek in *Concepts of Criticism*, pp. 128–221, is scarcely helpful. A promising but still shaky theorization of symbol, stemming from some Peircean insights, has been proposed by T. Todorov, 'Introduction à la Symbolique', in *Poétique*, 11.
21 Hall, *The Silent Language*.
22 Passmore, *A Hundred Years of Philosophy*, ch. 13.
23 The laconic chapter (ch. II) on symbol as a 'key to human nature' in his *An Essay on Man* bears witness to this plain generalism. Symbol is here only an anti-intellectualistic Ersatz for the definition of man as a rational being (Langer, of course, was to overstate this anti-intellectualistic note), and then (in the next chapter) of the general symbolic function we took care to distinguish from symbolization stricto sensu. Sperber, *Rethinking Symbolism*, p. 146–7, holds the same view: he notes that authors like Cassirer, Piaget and Lévi-Strauss equate symbolism with something larger than it, the conceptual mechanism as a whole. I would qualify this statement as far as Lévi-Strauss is concerned. In so far as he studies symbolism in myth and 'totemism', the symbolic is for him tantamount to the 'pensée sauvage'. Now the latter, while being not a bit less logic than our analytical reason (since it is not the 'pensée des sauvages', but the 'pensée à l'état sauvage'), follows a very different course: it is synthetic as well as analytical, semantic as well as quantifying, and is not ruled by a Zweckrationalität,

an instrumental, pragmatic rationality. To that extent, Lévi-Straussian symbolism is not simply dissolved into the conceptual mechanism—rather, it is a specialism within it. See *La Pensée sauvage*, pp. 289–90, 355.

24 Rieff, *The Triumph of the Therapeutic*, ch. 5, passim.

25 The significance of symbolic strategies set up by power groups has just been convincingly re-stated by Abner Cohen's *Two-Dimensional Man: An Essay on the Anthropology of Power and Symbolism in Complex Society*. Nowadays, as Cohen pithily wrote, 'ethnography is no longer news' (p. 10), and anthropology begins to accept intellectually, if not ethically, the ineluctable disappearance of segmental, the shrinking of traditional, society; therefore it becomes increasingly easier to realize that anthropology is committed to microsociological levels only in its techniques, not in its theoretial scope—a view forcefully asserted by Firth in his *Elements of Social Organization* (p. 18). Here, if anywhere, I feel inclined to add, lies the usefulness of the *second* 'revolution in anthropology' (to borrow Jarvie's catching formula) brought about by structuralism. After Lévi-Strauss, it is indeed much less likely for a good anthropologist to utterly forget the irreducibility of ethnology to ethnography. Evans-Pritchard's claim (in his *Social Anthropology*) that anthropologists' concern is with 'problems, not peoples', could still fall flat; Geertz's remark that they 'don't study villages—they study *in* villages' (*The Interpretation of Cultures*, p. 22) seems destined to a much brighter future.

26 Turner, *The Forest of Symbols*, p. 50.

27 Sperber, *Rethinking Symbolism*, pp. 18, 21.

28 Ibid., p. 23.

29 Ibid., p. 47.

30 Lévi-Strauss, 'The structural study of myth', reprinted in *Structural Anthropology*, ch. XI, whence comes also the sentence quoted.

31 Sperber, op. cit., pp. 57–9, 68–72, 82–4.

32 This kind of Chomskyan objection to Lévi-Strauss's myth theory amounts to a reversal of Sperber's own previous views; see his essay, 'Le Structuralisme en Anthropologie', in Ducrot et al., *Qu'est-ce que le structuralisme?*, pp. 207–8.

33 Sperber, *Rethinking Symbolism*, chs 4, 5.

34 Mukarowsky, *La Funzione, la Norma e il Valore Estetico come Fatti Sociali* (translated from the original Czech), pp. 37–8, 140.

35 Maurice Bloch, review of *Rethinking Symbolism*, in *Man*, pp. 128–9.

36 Sperber, op. cit., p. 137–9.

37 See Peirce, *Collected Papers*, vol. II; for a similar perspective (with very different terminology) see Prieto, 'Sémiologie', in *Encyclopédie de la Pléiade*, vol. *Langage*, pp. 94–5; and *Messages et signaux*, pp. 15–16; and Mounin, *Introduction à la sémiologie*, pp. 11–15.

38 Martinet, 'Connotations, poésie et culture', in Martinet et al., *To Honor Roman Jakobson*, vol. 2, p. 1, 288.

39 Eco, *Le Forme del Contenuto*, p. 59.

40 Panofsky, *Studies in Iconology*, ch. 1, and *Meaning Visual Arts*, ch. 1. On Panofsky's epistemological presuppositions and methodology see

Merquior, 'Analyse structurale des mythes et analyse des oeuvres d'art', in *L'Esthétique de Lévi-Strauss*.

Bibliography

Note: Books marked with an asterisk, though generally too recent for mention in the text, have been found, nevertheless, very pertinent to the discussion.

Adorno, Theodor W., *Minima Moralia: Reflections from Damaged Life* (1951), trans. E. F. N. Jephcott, London: New Left Books, 1974.
— *Prisms* (1955), trans. Samuel and Shierry Weber, London: Neville Spearman, 1967.
— *Negative Dialectics* (1966), trans. E. B. Ashton, London: Routledge & Kegan Paul, 1973.
Adorno, Theodor W., Frenkel-Brunswick, Else, Levinson, Daniel J., and Sanford, R. Nevitt, *The Authoritarian Personality*, New York: Harper & Bros, 1950.
Adorno, Theodor W. *et al., The Positivist Dispute in German Sociology*, trans. Glyn Adey and David Frisby, London: Heinemann, 1976.
Althusser, Louis, *For Marx* (1965), English trans., London: New Left Books, 1969.
— *Lenin and Philosophy and other Essays* (1971), English trans., London: New Left Books, 1971.
— *Réponse à John Lewis*, Paris: Maspéro, 1973.
— *Philosophie et philosophie spontanée des savants*, Paris: Maspéro, 1974.
— *Eléments d'autocritique*, Paris: Hachette, 1974.
Althusser, Louis and Balibar, Etienne, *Reading Capital* (1965), London: New Left Books, 1970.
Anderson, Perry, *Considerations on Western Marxism*, London: New Left Books, 1976.
Arendt, Hannah, *The Human Condition*, University of Chicago Press, 1958.
— *Between Past and Future*, New York: Viking Press, 1968 (1st edn., 1954).
— *On Violence*, London: Allen Lane, 1970.

Aron, Raymond, *D'une sainte famille à l'autre: essais sur les marxismes imaginaires*, Paris: Gallimard, 1969.
— *Plaidoyer pour l'Europe décadente*, Paris: Laffont, 1977.
*Augé, Marc, *Symbole, fonction, histoire*, Paris: Hachette, 1979.
*Avineri, Shlomo (ed.), *Varieties of Marxism*, The Hague: Nijhoff, 1977.
Ayer, A. J., *The Central Questions of Philosophy*, Harmondsworth: Pelican, 1976 (1st edn., 1973).
Bachelard, Gaston, *Le Nouvel Esprit scientifique* (1934), Paris: Presses Universitaires de France, 1975.
— *La Poétique de l'espace*, Paris: Presses Universitaires de France, 1957.
Bachrach, Peter and Baratz, Morton, S., *Power and Poverty—Theory and Practice*, Oxford University Press, 1970.
Barbu, Zevedei, *Society, Culture and Personality: An Introduction to Social Science*, Oxford: Blackwell, 1971.
Barnard, F. M., *Herder's Social and Political Thought: From Enlightenment to Nationalism*, Oxford: Clarendon Press, 1965.
*Barnes, Barry, *Interests and the Growth of Knowledge*, London: Routledge & Kegan Paul, 1977.
Barthes, Roland, *Mythologies* (A selection from *Mythologies*, Paris, 1957), trans. by Annette Lavers, London: Cape, 1972.
— *Critical Essays*, trans. Richard Howard, Evanston, Illinois: Northwestern Universities Press, 1972.
— *Système de la mode*, Paris, Seuil, 1967.
Bastide, Roger, *Sociologie et psychanalyse*, Paris: Presses Universitaires de France, 1972 (1st edn., 1950).
Bateson, Gregory, *Naven*, Stanford University Press, 2nd edn., 1958.
— *Steps to an Ecology of Mind*, Frogmore, St Albans: Paladin, 1973.
Bauman, Zygmunt, *Culture as Praxis*, London: Routledge & Kegan Paul, 1973.
—* *Towards a Critical Sociology: An Essay on Commonsense and Emancipation*, London: Routledge & Kegan Paul, 1976.
Bell, Daniel, *The Cultural Contradictions of Capitalism*, London: Heinemann, 1976.
Benoist, Jean-Marie, *La Révolution structurale*, Paris: Grasset, 1976.
Benveniste, Émile, *Problèmes de linguistique générale*, Paris: Gallimard, 1966.
— *Problèmes de linguistique générale II*, Paris: Gallimard, 1974.
Bergson, Henri, *Oeuvres*, Edition du Centenaire, Paris: Presses Universitaires de France, 1959.
Berlin, Isaiah, *Vico and Herder: Two Studies on the History of Ideas*, London: Hogarth Press, 1976.
Bernstein, Basil, *Class, Codes and Control*, London: Routledge & Kegan Paul, 1971.
*Bernstein, Richard J., *The Restructuring of Social and Political Theory*, Oxford: Blackwell, 1976.
Bidney, David, *Theoretical Anthropology*, Columbia University Press, 1953.
Bierstedt, Robert, *Power and Progress: Essays on Sociological Theory*, New York: McGraw-Hill, 1974.

Birnbaum, Norman, *Toward a Critical Sociology*, Oxford University Press, 1971.

Black, Max (ed.), *The Social Theories of Talcott Parsons: A Critical Examination*, Carbondale and Edwardsville: Southern Illinois University Press, 2nd edn., 1976.

Blau, Peter, *Exchange and Power in Social Life*, New York: John Wiley, 1964.

Bloch, Ernst, *Le Principe espérance*, trans. from Parts I, II and III of *Das Prinzip Hoffnung* (Frankfurt, 1959) by F. Wuilmart, Paris: Gallimard, 1976.

Bloch, Maurice (ed.), *Marxist Analyses and Social Anthropology*, London: Malaby Press, 1975.

Bocock, Robert, *Freud and Modern Society: An Outline and Analysis of Freud's Sociology*, Sunbury-on-Thames: Nelson, 1976.

Bolgar, R. R., *The Classical Heritage and Its Beneficiaries*, Cambridge University Press, 1954 (reprinted 1973).

Bottomore, T. B., *Sociology as Social Criticism*, London: Allen & Unwin, 1975.

Boudon, Raymond, *Les Méthodes en sociologie*, Paris: Presses Universitaires de France, 1969.

— *La Logique du social—introduction à la sociologie*, Paris: Hachette, 1979.

Bourdieu, Pierre, *Outline of a Theory of Practice*, trans. by Richard Nice, Cambridge University Press, 1977.

Braithwaite, R. B., *Scientific Explanation*, Cambridge University Press, 1953.

Bramson, Leon, *The Political Context of Sociology*, Princeton University Press, 1961.

Brinkmann, Carl, *Wirtschaftsformen und Lebensformen*, 1950.

*Brittan, Arthur, *The Privatised World*, London: Routledge & Kegan Paul, 1977.

Brodbeck, May (ed.), *Readings in the Philosophy of the Social Sciences*, London: Macmillan, 1968.

Brohm, Jean-Marie *et al., Contre Althusser*, Paris: 10/18, 1974.

Brown, L. B., *Ideology*, Harmondsworth: Penguin, 1973.

Buckley, Walter, *Sociology and Modern Systems Theory*, Englewood-Cliffs: Prentice-Hall, 1967.

Buhler, Karl, *Sprachtheorie*, Jena: Fischer, 1934; Spanish trans., Madrid, 1950.

Burke, Kenneth, *Philosophy of Literary Form*, Baton Rouge: Louisiana State University, 1941.

— *A Grammar of Motives*, Englewood-Cliffs: Prentice-Hall, 1945.

— *A Rhetoric of Motives*, Englewood-Cliffs: Prentice-Hall, 1950.

*Burns, Tom R. and Buckley, Walter (eds), *Power and Control: Social Structures and Their Transformation*, London: Sage, 1976.

Burrow, J. W., *Evolution and Society: A Study in Victorian Social Theory*, Cambridge University Press, 1966.

Callinicos, Alex, *Althusser's Marxism*, London: Pluto Press, 1976.

Canguilhem, Georges, *La Formation du concept de réflexe aux XVIIe et XVIIIe siècles*, Paris: Presses Universitaires de France, 1955.

Carlton, Eric, *Ideology and Social Order*, London, Routledge & Kegan Paul, 1977.

Carnap, Rudolf, *Philosophical Foundations of Physics: An Introduction to the Philosophy of Science*, ed. by Martin Gardner, New York: Basic Books, 1966.

*Carroll, John, *Break-Out from the Crystal Palace: The Anarcho-Psychological Critique: Stirner, Nietzsche, Dostoevsky*, London: Routledge & Kegan Paul, 1974.

Cassirer, Ernst, *Philosophy of Symbolic Forms*, trans. Ralph Mannheim, New Haven: Yale University Press, 1953–7 (3 vols).

Cavaillès, Jean, *Sur la logique et la théorie de la science*, Paris: 1947.

Chaunu, Pierre, *Le Temps des réformes: La crise de la chrétienté: l'éclatement (1250–1550)*, Paris: Fayard, 1975.

Chodak, Szymon, *Societal Development: Five Approaches with Conclusions from Comparative Analysis*, New York: Oxford University Press, 1973.

Chomsky, Noam, *Cartesian Linguistics: A Chapter in the History of Rationalist Thought*, New York: Harper & Row, 1966.

Cicourel, Aaron V., *Cognitive Sociology: Language and Meaning in Social Interaction*, Harmondsworth: Penguin, 1973.

Clastres, Pierre, *La Société contre l'état*, Paris: Minuit, 1974.

Cobban, Alfred, *Aspects of the French Revolution*, Frogmore, St Albans: Paladin, 2nd edn., 1971.

Cochrane, Charles Norris, *Christianity and Classical Culture: A Study of Thought and Action from Augustus to Augustine*, Oxford University Press, 1974 (1st edn., 1940).

Cohen, Abner, *Two-Dimensional Man: An Essay on the Anthropology of Power and Symbolism in Complex Society*, London: Routledge & Kegan Paul, 1974.

Cohen, Percy S., *Modern Social Theory*, London: Heinemann, 1968.

Cohen, Yehudi (ed.), *Man in Adaptation: The Institutional Framework*, Chicago: Aldine-Atherton Press, 1971.

Cohn, Gabriel, *Sociologia da Comunicação: Teoria e Ideologia*, Sao Paulo: Pioneira, 1973.

Colletti, Lucio, *From Rousseau to Lenin (Ideologia e Società)*, trans. by John Merrington and Judith White, London: New Left Books, 1972.

*Coser, Lewis A. (ed.), *The Idea of Social Structure: Papers in Honor of R. K. Merton*, New York: Harcourt Brace, 1975.

Curtius, Ernst Robert, *European Literature and the Latin Middle Ages*, trans. from the German original (Bern, 1948) by W. Trask, London: Pantheon Books, 1953.

Dahl, Robert, *Who Governs?*, New Haven: Yale University Press, 1961.

Dahrendorf, Ralf, *Essays in the Theory of Society*, London: Routledge & Kegan Paul, 1968.

Davidson, Donald and Harman, Gilbert (eds), *Semantics of Natural Languages*, Dordrecht and Boston: Reidel, 2nd edn., 1972.

Demerath III, N. J. and Peterson, Richard A. (eds), *System, Change, and Conflict: A Reader on Contemporary Sociological Theory and the Debate over Functionalism*, New York: Free Press, 1967.

Dilthey, Wilhelm, *Pattern and Meaning in History: Thoughts on History and Society* (partial trans. of *Der Aufbau der geschichtlichen Welt in den Geisteswissenschaften*), ed. by H. P. Rickman, New York: Harper & Row, 1962.

Dole, Gertrude and Carneiro, Robert (eds), *Essays in the Science of Culture in Honor of Leslie A. White*, New York: Crowell, 1960.

Douglas, Mary, *Purity and Danger: An Analysis of the Concepts of Pollution and Taboo*, London: Routledge & Kegan Paul, 1966.

Ducrot, Oswald *et al., Qu'est-ce que le structuralisme?*, Paris: Seuil, 1968.

Duhem, Pierre, *To Save the Phenomena*, trans. E. Doland and C. Maschler, University of Chicago Press, 1969.

*Dumont, Louis, *Homo Aequalis: genèse et épanouissement de l'idéologie économique*, Paris: Gallimard, 1977.

Durkheim, Emile, *Selected Writings*, ed. and trans. by Anthony Giddens, Cambridge University Press, 1972.

— *The Elementary Forms of the Religious Life*, trans. Joseph Ward Swaine, London: Allen & Unwin (1st edn., 1915).

Easton, David, *A Systems Analysis of Political Life*, New York: Wiley, 1965.

Eco, Humberto, *Le Forme del Contenuto*, Milan: Bompiani, 1971.

Eisenstadt, S. N. and Curelaru, M., *The Form of Sociology: Paradigms and Crises*, New York: Wiley, 1976.

Ekeh, Peter, *Social Exchange Theory: The Two Traditions*, London: Heinemann, 1974.

*Eldridge, J. E. T., *Sociology and Industrial Life*, Sunbury-on-Thames: Nelson, 1971.

Elias, Norbert, *La Civilisation des moeurs*, trans. of vol. 1 of *Über den Prozess der Zivilisation* (1939), by Pierre Kamnitzer, Paris: Calmann-Lévy, 1973.

Etzioni, Amitai, *The Active Society: A Theory of Societal and Political Processes*, New York: Free Press, 1968.

Evans-Pritchard, E. E., *Social Anthropology*, London: Routledge & Kegan Paul, 1972 (1st edn., 1951).

Febvre, Lucien and Martin, Henri-Jean, *The Coming of the Book: The Impact of Printing 1450–1800*, trans., David Gerard, London: New Left Books, 1976.

Feidelson, Charles Jr, *Symbolism and American Literature*, Chicago University Press, 1953.

Fernandes, Florestan, *Fundamentos Empiricos da Explicação Sociológica*, São Paulo: Nacional, 1967.

Feuer, Lewis S., *Ideology and the Ideologists*, Oxford: Blackwell, 1975.

Feyerabend, Paul, *Against Method: Outline of an Anarchistic Theory of Knowledge*, London: New Left Books, 1975.

Finer, Samuel E., *Comparative Government*, Harmondsworth: Pelican, 1974 (2nd impression).

Firth, Raymond, *Elements of Social Organization*, London: Tavistock,

1971 (1st edn., 1951).
— *Symbols: Public and Private*, London: Allen & Unwin, 1973.
Fodor, Jerry A. and Katz, Jerrold J., *The Structure of Language: Reading in the Philosophy of Language*, Englewood Cliffs: Prentice-Hall, 1964.
Fortes, Meyer, *Kinship and the Social Order*, London: Routledge & Kegan Paul, 1969.
Foucault, Michel, *The Order of Things: An Archaeology of the Human Sciences*, trans. from *Les Mots et les Choses* (Paris, 1966), London: Tavistock, 1970.
Freud, Sigmund, *Civilization and its Discontents*, Standard Edition by James Strachey et al., vol. XXI, London: Hogarth Press, 1963.
— *New Introductory Lectures on Psychoanalysis*, Standard Edition by James Strachey et al., vol. XXII, London: Hogarth Press, 1962.
Friedrich, Carl Joachim, *Man and his Government: An Empirical Theory of Politics*, New York: McGraw-Hill, 1963.
— *Tradition and Authority*, London: Macmillan, 1972.
Frye, Northrop, *Anatomy of Criticism*, Princeton University Press, 1957.
— *The Secular Scripture*, New York: Harvard University Press, 1976.
Gabel, Joseph, *Idéologies*, Paris: Anthropos, 1974.
Gadamer, Hans Georg, *Truth and Method*, translation by G. Barden and J. Cumming of the 2nd edn. of *Wahrheit und Methode* (Tübingen, 1965), London: Sheed & Ward, 1975.
— *Philosophical Hermeneutics*, translation of a selection of essays from *Kleine Schriften* (3 vols) by David E. Linge, Berkeley: University of California Press, 1976.
Gardner, Howard, *The Quest for Mind: Piaget, Lévi-Strauss and the Structuralist Movement*, New York: Knopf, 1973; London: Quartet, 1976.
Garfinkel, H., *Studies in Ethnomethodology*, Englewood Cliffs: Prentice-Hall, 1967.
Gay, Peter, *Art and Act: On Causes in History*, New York: Harper & Row, 1976.
Geertz, Clifford, *The Interpretation of Cultures*, London: Hutchinson, 1975 (1st edn., 1973).
Gellner, Ernest, *Thought and Change*, London: Weidenfeld & Nicolson, 1964.
— *Cause and Meaning in the Social Sciences*, London: Routledge & Kegan Paul, 1973.
— *Contemporary Thought and Politics*, London: Routledge & Kegan Paul, 1974.
— *The Devil in Modern Philosophy*, London: Routledge & Kegan Paul, 1974.
— *Legitimation of Belief*, Cambridge University Press, 1974.
Giddens, Anthony, *Capitalism and Modern Social Theory*, Cambridge University Press, 1971.
— *The Class Structure of Advanced Societies*, London: Hutchinson, 1973.
Godelier, Maurice, *Horizon, trajets marxistes en anthropologie*, Paris: Maspéro, 1977 (1st edn., 1973), 2 vols.

Bibliography

Goffman, Erving, *The Presentation of the Self in Everyday Life*, New York: Doubleday, 1959.

Gouldner, Alvin W., *The Coming Crisis of Western Sociology*, New York: Basic Books, 1970.

— *For Sociology: Renewal and Critique in Sociology Today*, Harmondsworth: Pelican, 1975 (1st edn., 1973).

— *The Dialectic of Ideology and Technology: The Origins, Grammar and Future of Ideology*, London: Macmillan, 1976.

Gouldner, Alvin W. and Peterson, Richard, *Notes on Technology and the Moral Order*, New York: Bobbs-Merrill, 1962.

Gramsci, Antonio, *Selections from the Prison Notebooks*, ed. and trans. by Q. Hoare and G. Nowell-Smith, London: Lawrence and Wishart, 1971.

Gross, Llewelyn (ed.), *Symposium on Sociological Theory*, New York: Harper & Row, 1959.

Habermas, Jürgen, *Strukturwandel der Oeffentlichkeit*, Neuwied: Luchterhand, 1962. Italian translation as *Storia e critica dell'opinione pubblica*, Bari: Laterza, 1971.

— *Zur Logik der Sozialwissenschaften*, Tübingen: Mohr, 1967. Italian translation as *Logica della Scienze Sociale*, Bologna: Il Mulino, 1970.

— *Technik und Wissenschaft als Ideologie*, Frankfurt: Suhrkamp, 1968. Italian translation as *Teoria e Prassi nella Società Tecnologica*, Bari: Laterza, 1969.

— *Knowledge and Human Interests*, London: Heinemann, 1972. Translation of *Erkenntnis und Interesse* (Frankfurt, 1968) by Jeremy Shapiro.

— 'Toward a theory of communicative competence', in H. P. Dreitzel (ed.), *Recent Sociology*, vol. 2, New York: Macmillan, 1970.

— *Toward a Rational Society: Student Protest, Science and Politics*, translation of *Protestbewegung und Hochschulreform* (Frankfurt, 1969) by J. Shapiro, London: Heinemann, 1972.

— *Theory and Practice*, trans. by John Viertel (German original, 1963), London: Heinemann, 1974.

— *Legitimation Crisis*, trans. by Thomas McCarthy of *Legitimationsprobleme im Spätkapitalismus* (Frankfurt, 1973), Boston: Beacon Press, 1975.

Hall, Edward T., *The Silent Language*, Greenwich, Connecticut: Fawcett, 1961 (1st edn., 1951).

— *Beyond Culture*, New York: Doubleday, 1976.

Hamilton, Peter, *Knowledge and Social Structure: An Introduction to the Classical Argument in the Sociology of Knowledge*, London: Routledge & Kegan Paul, 1974.

*Hanson, F. Allan, *Meaning in Culture*, London: Routledge & Kegan Paul, 1975.

Harman, Gilbert (ed.), *On Noam Chomsky: Critical Essays*, New York: Doubleday, 1974.

Harré, Rom, *An Introduction to the Logic of the Sciences*, London: Macmillan, 1967.

— *The Philosophies of Science: An Introductory Survey*, Oxford University Press, 1972.

Harris, Marvin, *The Rise of Anthropological Theory: A History of Theories of Culture*, New York: Crowell, 1968.

Hawkes, Terence, *Structuralism and Semiotics*, London: Methuen, 1977.

*Hawthorn, Geoffrey, *Enlightenment and Despair: A History of Sociology*, Cambridge University Press, 1976.

Hayek, Friedrich von, *The Counter-Revolution of Science: A Study on the Abuse of Reason*, Chicago: Free Press; London: Collier Macmillan, 1955 (1st edn., 1952).

— *Studies in Philosophy, Politics, Economics*, London: Routledge & Kegan Paul, 1967.

— **New Studies in Philosophy, Politics, Economics and the History of Ideas*, London: Routledge & Kegan Paul, 1978.

Hegel, Georg Wilhelm Friedrich, *The Phenomenology of Mind* (1807), translation of *Phänomenologie des Geistes* by J. B. Baillie, London: Allen & Unwin, 1931 (2nd edn.), 2 vols.

— *Science of Logic*, trans. W. H. Johnston and L. G. Struthers, London: Allen & Unwin, 1929, 2 vols.

— *Jenenser Realphilosophie*, Leipzig: Meiner, 1932, 2 vols.

Heidegger, Martin, *Being and Time*, trans. John Macquarrie and Edward Robinson, London: SCM, 1962.

— *Introduction to Metaphysics*, trans. Ralph Mannheim, New Haven: Yale University Press, 1958.

— *Existence and Being*, several translations ed. by Werner Brock, Chicago: Regnery, 1949.

— *The End of Philosophy*, trans. from vol. II of *Nietzsche* (Pfullingen, 1961), by Joan Stambaugh, New York: Harper & Row, 1973.

Hempel, Carl, *Aspects of Scientific Explanation and Other Essays in the Philosophy of Science*, New York: Free Press, 1965.

Herder, Johann Gottfried, *Idées pour la philosophie de l'histoire de l'humanité*, selections trans. by M. Rouché, Paris: Aubier, 1962.

— *On Social and Political Culture*, ed. and trans. by F. M. Barnard, Cambridge University Press, 1969.

Heusch, Luc de, *Pourquoi l'épouser? et autres essais*, Paris: Gallimard, 1971.

Highet, Gilbert, *The Classical Tradition: Greek and Roman Influences on Western Literature*, Oxford University Press, 1949.

Hirschman, Albert O., *The Passions and the Interests: Political Arguments for Capitalism Before its Triumph*, Princeton University Press, 1977.

Hjelmslev, Louis, *Prolegomena to a Theory of Language,* (*Omkring sprogteoriens grundlaeggelse*) trans. F. J. Whitfield, Madison: University of Wisconsin Press, 1963.

Hobsbawm, Eric, *The Age of Revolution: Europe 1789–1848*, London: Weidenfeld & Nicolson, 1962.

Homans, George Gaspar, *Social Behaviour: Its Elementary Forms*, New York: Harcourt, Brace & World, 1961.

Hondt, Jacques d', *De Hegel à Marx*, Paris: Presses Universitaires de France, 1972.
— *L'Idéologie de la rupture*, Paris: Presses Universitaires de France, 1978.
Horkheimer, Max, *The Eclipse of Reason*, New York: Oxford University Press, 1947.
— *Critical Theory: Selected Essays*, trans. Matthew J. O'Connell *et al.*, New York: Seabury Press, n.d.
Horkheimer, Max and Adorno, T. W., *Dialektik der Aufklärung*, Amsterdam: Querido, 1947; trans. as *Dialectic of Enlightenment*, London: Allen Lane, 1973.
*Howard, Dick, *The Marxian Legacy*, London: Macmillan, 1977.
Hudson, Liam, *Frames of Mind*, London: Methuen, 1968.
Huntington, Samuel P., *Political Order in Changing Societies*, New Haven: Yale University Press, 1968.
Husserl, Edmund, *The Crisis of European Sciences and Transcendental Phenomenology*, trans. David Carr, Evanston: Northwestern University Press, 1970.
Jaeger, Werner, *Early Christianity and Greek Paideia*, Oxford University Press, 1969 (1st edn., 1961).
Jaguaribe, Helio, *Political Development: A General Theory and a Latin American Case Study*, New York: Harper & Row, 1973.
Jakubowski, Franz, *Ideology and Superstructure in Historical Materialism*, trans. Anne Booth, London: Allison & Busby, 1976.
Jameson, Fredric, *Marxism and Form,* Princeton University Press, 1971.
— *The Prison-House of Language: A Critical Account of Structuralism and Russian Formalism*, Princeton University Press, 1972.
Jarvie, I. C., *Concepts and Society*, London: Routledge & Kegan Paul, 1972.
Jay, Martin, *The Dialectical Imagination: A History of the Frankfurt School and the Institute of Social Research 1923–50*, London: Heinemann, 1973.
Jones, Gareth Stedman et al., *Western Marxism: A Critical Reader*, London: New Left Books, 1977.
Kant, Immanuel, *Critique of Pure Reason*, trans. Norman Kemp Smith, London: Macmillan, 1958.
— *On History*, essays ed. by Lewis White Beck, Indianapolis: Bobbs-Merrill, 1963.
Kaplan, David and Manners, Robert A., *Culture Theory*, Englewood Cliffs: Prentice-Hall, 1972.
Kelley, Donald R., *Foundations of Modern Historical Scholarship*, Columbia University Press, 1970.
Kolakowski, Leszek, *Toward a Marxist Humanism: Essays on the Left Today*, trans. Jane Z. Peel, New York: Grove Press, 1968.
Kolakowski, Leszek and Hampshire, Stuart (eds), *The Socialist Idea: A Reappraisal*, London: Quartet Books, 1977 (1st edn., 1974).
Koyrè, Alexandre, *Etudes galiléennes*, Paris: Hermann, 1939–40, 3 vols.
Kroeber, A. L., *Anthropology: Culture, Patterns and Processes*, New York: Harcourt, Brace & World, 1963 (1st edn., 1923, revised 1948).

Kroeber, A. L. and Kluckhohn, Clyde, *Culture: A Critical Review of Concepts and Definitions*, Harvard University Press, 1952.

Kuhn, Thomas, *The Structure of Scientific Revolutions*, University of Chicago Press, 1962.

Kuper, Adam, *Anthropologists and Anthropology: The British School 1922–72*, London: Allen Lane, 1973; Harmondsworth: Penguin, 1975.

Kurtz, Paul (ed.), *American Philosophy in the Twentieth Century: A Sourcebook from Pragmatism to Philosophical Analysis*, New York: Macmillan, 1966.

*Laclau, Ernesto, *Politics and Ideology in Marxist Theory*, London: New Left Books, 1977.

Lakatos, Imre and Musgrave, Alan, *Criticism and the Growth of Knowledge*, Cambridge University Press, 1970.

Landes, David S., *The Unbound Prometheus: Technological Change and Industrial Development in Western Europe from 1750 to the Present*, Cambridge University Press, 1969.

Lane, R. E., *Political Ideology*, New York: Free Press, 1962.

Lapassade, Georges and Lourau, X., *Clefs pour la sociologie*, Paris: Seghers 1970.

Laslett, Peter and Runciman, W. G. (eds), *Philosophy, Politics and Society*, 1st series, 1956; 2nd series, 1962; 3rd series, 1969, Oxford: Blackwell.

Laslett, Peter, Runciman, W. G. and Skinner, Q. (eds), *Philosophy, Politics and Society* (4th Series), Oxford: Blackwell, 1972.

Lazarsfeld, Paul, *Qualitative Analysis: Historical and Critical Essays*, Boston: Allyn & Bacon, 1972.

Leach, E. R., *Rethinking Anthropology*, London: Athlone Press, 1971 (1st edn., 1961).

*Lehman, Edward W., *Political Society: A Macrosociology of Politics*, New York: Columbia University Press, 1977.

Leinfellner, Werner and Köhler, Eckehart, *Developments in the Methodology of Social Science*, Dordrecht and Boston: Reidel, 1974.

Lenski, Gerhard E., *Power and Privilege: A Theory of Social Stratification*, New York: McGraw-Hill, 1966.

Lepschy, Giulio C., *La Linguistica Strutturale*, Turin: Einaudi, 1966.

Leroi-Gourhan, André, *Le Geste et la parole,* Paris: Albin Michel, 1964, 2 vols.

Levison, Arnold B., *Knowledge and Society: An Introduction to the Philosophy of the Social Sciences*, Indianapolis and New York: Bobbs-Merrill, 1974.

Lévi-Strauss, Claude, 'Introduction à l'oeuvre de Marcel Mauss', in Marcel Mauss, *Sociologie et anthropologie*, Paris: Presses Universitaires de France, 1950.

— *Structural Anthropology*, trans. C. Jocobson and B. G. Schoepf, New York: Basic Books, 1963.

— *The Savage Mind*, Chicago University Press, 1966.

— *The Raw and the Cooked*, trans. by John and Doreen Weightman of *Mythologiques I*, London: Cape, 1970.

— *From Honey to Ashes*, trans. by J. D. Weightman of *Mythologiques II*,

London: Cape, 1973.
— *L'Origine des manières de table* (*Mythologiques III*), Paris: Plon, 1968.
— *L'Homme nu* (*Mythologiques IV*), Paris: Plon, 1971.
— *Anthropologie structurale II*, Paris: Plon, 1973.
Lewis, I. M., *Social Anthropology in Perspective: The Relevance of Social Anthropology*, Harmondsworth: Penguin, 1976.
Lichtheim, George, *Marxism: An Historical and Critical Study*, London: Routledge & Kegan Paul, 1964 (1st edn., 1961).
— *The Concept of Ideology and Other Essays*, New York: Vintage Books, 1967.
— *From Marx to Hegel and Other Essays*, London: Orbach & Chambers, 1971.
*Lindblom, Charles E., *Politics and Markets: The World's Political Economic Systems*, New York: Basic Books, 1977.
Lipset, Seymour Martin, *Political Man: The Social Bases of Politics*, London: Heinemann, 1963 (1st edn., 1959).
Loewith, Karl, *From Hegel to Nietzsche*, trans. of the German edn. (Zurich, 1949), London: Constable, 1965.
— *Meaning in History*, University of Chicago Press, 1970 (1st edn., 1949).
Losee, John, *A Historical Introduction to the Philosophy of Science*, Oxford University Press, 1972.
Luhmann, Niklas, *Legitimation durch Verfahren*, Neuwied: Luchterhand, 1969.
Lukacs, Georg, *History and Class Consciousness*, trans. R. Livingstone, London: Merlin Press, 1971.
Lukes, Steven, *Emile Durkheim: His Life and Work: A Historical and Critical Study*, Harmondsworth: Penguin, 1975 (1st edn., 1973).
— *Individualism*, Oxford: Blackwell, 1973.
— *Power: A Radical View*, London: Macmillan, 1974.
— *Essays in Social Theory*, London: Macmillan, 1977.
Mach, Ernst, *The Analysis of Sensations*, trans. C. M. Williams, New York: Dover, 1959.
Macintyre, Alastair C., *Against the Self-Images of the Age*, London: Duckworth, 1971.
Macpherson, C. B., *The Real World of Democracy*, Oxford: Clarendon, 1965.
— *Democratic Theory: Essays in Retrieval*, Oxford: Clarendon, 1973.
— *The Life and Times of Liberal Democracy*, Oxford University Press, 1977.
MacRae, Donald G., *Ideology and Society*, London: Heinemann, 1961.
Malinowski, Bronislaw, *A Scientific Theory of Culture*, Chapel Hill: University of North Carolina Press, 1944.
Manners, Robert A. and Kaplan, David, *Theory in Anthropology*, Chicago: Aldine, 1968.
Mannheim, Karl, *Ideology and Utopia*, London: Routledge & Kegan Paul, 1960 (1st edn., 1936).
— *Essays on the Sociology of Knowledge*, London: Routledge & Kegan Paul, 1952.

— *Essays on Sociology and Social Psychology*, London: Routledge & Kegan Paul, 1953.
— *Essays on the Sociology of Culture*, London: Routledge & Kegan Paul, 1956.
Manuel, Frank E., *Shapes of Philosophical History*, Stanford University Press, 1965.
Marcuse, Herbert, *Eros and Civilization: A Philosophical Inquiry into Freud*, Boston: Beacon Press, 1955.
— *One-Dimensional Man: Studies in the Ideology of Advanced Industrial Society*, Boston: Beacon Press, 1964.
— *Negations: Essays in Critical Theory*, trans. by Jeremy Shapiro, London: Allen Lane, 1968.
Marrou, Henri Irenée, *Saint Augustin et la fin de la culture antique*, Paris: Ecoles Françaises d'Athènes et de Rome, 1938–49 (2 vols), 4th edn 1958.
Martin, Roderick, *The Sociology of Power*, London: Routledge & Kegan Paul, 1977.
Martindale, Don, *The Nature and Types of Sociological Theory*, London: Routledge & Kegan Paul, 1961.
— *Sociological Theory and the Problem of Values*, Columbus, Ohio: Merrill, 1974.
Martinet, A., *Eléments de linguistique générale*, Paris: A. Colin, 1960.
Martinet, A. et al., *To Honor Roman Jakobson*, Paris and The Hague: Mouton, 1967.
Marx, Karl, *Critique of Hegel's 'Philosophy of Right' (1843)*, trans. by Annette Jolin and Joseph O'Malley and ed. by the latter, Cambridge University Press, 1970.
— *Grundrisse: Foundations of the Critique of Political Economy*, trans. by Martin Nicolaus, Harmondsworth: Penguin, 1973.
— *Capital*, trans. by Ben Fowkes, Harmondsworth: Penguin, 1976.
— *Selected Writings in Sociology and Social Philosophy*, ed. by T. B. Bottomore and Maximilien Rubel and trans. by the former, London: Watts, 1961 (1st edn., 1956).
— *Writings of the Young Marx on Philosophy and Society*, ed. and trans. by Loyd D. Easton and Kurt H. Guddat, Garden City, New York: Doubleday, 1967.
Marx, Karl and Engels, Friedrich, *The German Ideology* (1845), London: Lawrence & Wishart, 1965.
Mead, George Herbert, *On Social Psychology*, ed. by Anselm Strauss, University of Chicago Press, 1956.
Medawar, Peter, *The Uniqueness of the Individual*, London: Methuen, 1957.
Meinecke, Friedrich, *Historism: The Rise of a New Historical Outlook*, trans. J. E. Anderson, London: Routledge & Kegan Paul, 1972.
Meltzer, Bernard N. et al., *Symbolic Interactionism: Genesis, Varieties and Criticism*, London: Routledge & Kegan Paul, 1975.
Menger, Carl, *Problems of Economics and Sociology*, trans. and ed. by Louis Schneider, University of Illinois Press, 1963.

Merleau-Ponty, Maurice, *Phenomenology of Perception*, trans. Colin Smith, New York: Humanities Press, 1962.
— *Signs*, trans. Richard McCleary, Evanston, Illinois: Northwestern University Press, 1964.
Merquior, J. G., *L'Esthétique de Lévi-Strauss*, Paris: Presses Universitaires de France, 1977.
— *Rousseau and Weber: Two Studies in the Theory of Legitimacy*, London: Routledge & Kegan Paul (forthcoming).
Merton, Robert K., *Social Theory and Social Structure*, enlarged edn, New York: Free Press, 1968.
Merton, R. K., Broom, Leonard and Cottrell, Leonard, *Sociology Today: Problems and Prospects*, New York: Basic Books, 1959.
Michaud, Guy, *Message poétique du symbolisme*, Paris: Nizet, 1947.
Mill, John Stuart, *A System of Logic*, (1843), London: Routledge & Kegan Paul, 1949; Longmans, 1970.
Mills, C. Wright, *The Power Elite*, New York: Oxford University Press, 1956.
— *The Sociological Imagination*, New York: Oxford University Press, 1959.
Moore, Barrington, *Social Origins of Dictatorship and Democracy: Lord and Peasant in the Making of the Modern World*, Boston: Beacon Press, 1976.
Morin, Edgar and Piattelli-Palmarini, Massimo (eds), *L'Unité de l'homme: Invariants biologiques et universaux culturels*, Paris: Seuil, 1974.
Moscovici, Serge, *La Société contre nature*, Paris: 10/18, 1972.
Mounin, Georges, *Introduction à la sémiologie*, Paris: Minuit, 1970.
Mueller, Claus, *The Politics of Communication: A Study in the Political Sociology of Language, Socialization and Legitimation*, New York: Oxford University Press, 1973.
Mukarowsky, Jan, *La Funzione, la Norma e il Valore Estetico come Fatti Sociali*, trans. from *Studie z estetiky* (Prague, 1966), Turin: Einaudi, 1971.
Nadel, S. F., *The Foundations of Social Anthropology*, London: Cohen & West, 1969 (1st edn, 1951).
— *The Theory of Social Structure*, London: Cohen & West, 1969 (1st edn, 1967).
Nagel, Ernest, *Logic Without Metaphysics and Other Essays in the Philosophy of Science*, Chicago, Illinois: Free Press, 1954.
— *The Structure of Science: Problems in the Logic of Scientific Explanation*, New York: Harcourt, Brace & World, 1961.
*Nagel, Jack, *The Descriptive Analysis of Power*, New Haven: Yale University Press, 1975.
Neale, R. S., *Class and Ideology in the Nineteenth Century*, London: Routledge & Kegan Paul, 1972.
Needham, Rodney, *Belief, Language, and Experience*, Oxford: Blackwell, 1972.
Negt, Oskar, *Politik als Protest*, Frankfurt: Suhrkamp, 1971.
Niedermann, Joseph, *Kultur: Werden und Wandlungen des Begriffes; und*

seiner Ersatzbegriffe von Cicero bis Herder, Florence: Bibliotheca dell' Archivum Romanum, vol. XXVIII, 1941.

Nietzsche, Friedrich, *On the Genealogy of Morals and Ecce Homo*, trans. by Walter Kaufmann, New York: Random House, 1969.

Nisbet, Robert Alexander, *The Sociological Tradition*, London: Heinemann, 1967.

— *Social Change and History: Aspects of the Western Theory of Development*, New York: Oxford University Press, 1969.

Nossiter, T. G. et al. (eds), *Imagination and Precision in the Social Sciences*, London: Faber, 1972.

Oberschall, Anthony (ed.), *The Establishment of Empirical Sociology: Studies in Continuity, Discontinuity, and Institutionalization*, New York: Harper & Row, 1972.

Offe, Claus, *Industry and Inequality*, London: Arnold, 1976.

O'Neill, John, *Sociology as a Skin Trade: Essays Towards a Reflexive Sociology*, London: Heinemann, 1972.

Panofsky, Erwin, *Studies in Iconology*, Oxford University Press, 1939.

— *Meaning in the Visual Arts*, New York: Doubleday, 1955.

Pareto, Vilfredo, *Sociological Writings*, trans. by Derick Mirfin and selected and introduced by Samuel I. Finer, Oxford: Blackwell, 1976 (1st edn, 1966).

Parkin, Frank, *Class Inequality and Political Order*, Frogmore, St Albans: Paladin, 1972.

Parry, Geraint, *Political Elites*, London: Allen & Unwin, 1969.

Parsons, Talcott, *The Structure of Social Action*, Chicago: Free Press, 1949 (1st edn., 1937).

— *The Social System*, Chicago: Free Press, 1951.

— *Essays in Sociological Theory*, Chicago: Free Press, 1954 (revised edn).

— *Politics and the Social Structure*, New York: Free Press, 1969.

— *Societies: Evolutionary and Comparative Perspectives*, Englewood Cliffs: Prentice-Hall, 1966.

— *The System of Modern Societies*, Englewood Cliffs: Prentice-Hall, 1971.

Parsons, Talcott, Bales, R. F. and Shils, E. A., *Working Papers in the Theory of Action*, Chicago: Free Press, 1953.

Parsons, Talcott and Shils, Edward A. (eds), *Toward a General Theory of Action: Theoretical Foundations for the Social Sciences*, New York: Harper & Row, 1962 (1st edn, 1951).

Passmore, John, *A Hundred Years of Philosophy*, Harmondsworth: Penguin, 1975 (1st edn, 1957).

Peacock, James L., *Consciousness and Change: Symbolic Anthropology in Evolutionary Perspective*, Oxford: Blackwell, 1975.

Peirce, Charles Sanders, *Collected Papers, Volume II*, ed. C. Hawthorne and P. Weiss, Cambridge, Mass.: Harvard University Press, 1960 (1st edn., 1932).

— *Selected Writings*, ed. Philip P. Wiener, New York: Dover, 1958.

— *The Essential Writings*, ed. Edward C. Moore, New York: Harper & Row, 1972.

Perkin, Harold, *The Origins of Modern English Society 1780–1880*, London:Routledge & Kegan Paul, 1969.

*Pfeiffer, Rudolf, *History of Classical Scholarship 1300–1850*, Oxford: Clarendon, 1976.

Piaget, Jean, *Introduction à l'épistémologie génétique, vol. III: la pensée biologique, la pensée psychologique et la pensée sociologique*, Paris: Presses Universitaires de France, 1950.

— *Etudes sociologiques*, Geneva: Droz, 1967.

Plamenatz, John, *Man and Society: Political and Social Theory*, New York: McGraw-Hill, 1963, 2 vols.

— *Ideology*, London: Macmillan, 1971 (1st edn., 1970).

— *Democracy and Illusion: An Examination of Certain Aspects of Modern Democratic Theory*, London: Longmans, 1973.

Pocock, J. G. A., *Politics, Language and Time: Essays on Political Thought and History*, London: Methuen, 1972 (1st edn., 1971).

Poggi, Gianfranco, *Images of Society: Essays on the Sociological Theories of Tocqueville, Marx, and Durkheim*, Stanford University Press, 1972.

Poirier, Jean (ed.), *Ethnologie générale*, Paris: Gallimard (Encyclopédie de la Pléiade), 1968.

Polanyi, Karl, *The Great Transformation: The Political and Economic Origins of Our Time*, Boston: Beacon Press, 1957 (1st edn., 1944).

Polanyi, Michael, *Personal Knowledge: Towards a Post-Critical Philosophy*, London: Routledge & Kegan Paul, 1973 (1st edn., 1958).

Popper, Karl Raimund, *The Logic of Scientific Discovery*, London: Hutchinson, 1974 (1st edn. in the German original, Vienna, 1934).

— *The Open Society and Its Enemies*, London: Routledge & Kegan Paul, 1966 (1st edn., 1945), 2 vols.

— *The Poverty of Historicism*, London: Routledge & Kegan Paul, 1957.

— *Conjectures and Refutations: The Growth of Scientific Knowledge*, London: Routledge & Kegan Paul, 1972 (1st edn., 1963).

— *Objective Knowledge: An Evolutionary Approach*, Oxford: Clarendon, 1975 (1st edn., 1972).

— *Unended Quest: An Intellectual Autobiography*, London: Fontana/ Collins, 1976 (1st edn., 1974).

Poulantzas, Nicos, *Political Power and Social Classes*, London: New Left Books, 1973 (1st French edn., Paris, 1968).

— *Classes in Contemporary Capitalism*, London: New Left Books, 1975 (1st French edn., Paris, 1974).

Quine, Willard Van Orman, *From a Logical Point of View*, New York: Harper & Row, 1963 (1st edn., 1953).

— *Word and Object*, Cambridge, Mass.: MIT Press, 1975 (1st edn., 1960).

Quine, W. V. and Ullian, J. S., *The Web of Belief*, New York: Random House, 1970.

Radcliffe-Brown, Alfred Reginald, *A Natural Science of Society*, Chicago: Free Press, 1957.

Radnitzky, Gerard, *Contemporary Schools of Metascience*, Göteborg: Akademiförlaget, 1970 (1st edn., 1968).

Rancière, Jacques, *La Leçon d'Althusser*, Paris: Gallimard, 1974.

Rawls, John, *A Theory of Justice*, Oxford University Press, 1972 (1st edn., 1971).

Reichenbach, Hans, *Experience and Prediction: An Analysis of the Foundations and Structure of Knowledge*, University of Chicago Press, 1938.

Rex, John, *Key Problems of Sociological Theory*, London: Routledge & Kegan Paul, 1973 (1st edn., 1961).

— *Sociology and the Demystification of the Modern World*, London: Routledge & Kegan Paul, 1974.

Rex, John (ed.), *Approaches to Sociology: An Introduction to Major Trends in British Sociology*, London: Routledge & Kegan Paul, 1974.

Rickert, Heinrich, *Science and History: A Critique of Positivist Anthropology*, trans. of *Kulturwissenschaft und Naturwissenschaft* (1899), Princeton University Press, 1962.

Riesman, David et al., *The Lonely Crowd*, New Haven: Yale University Press, 1950.

Rieff, Philip, *Freud: The Mind of the Moralist*, New York: Doubleday, 1961 (1st edn., 1959).

— *The Triumph of the Therapeutic*, Harmondsworth: Penguin, 1966.

*Robertson, Roland, *Meaning and Change: Explorations in the Cultural Sociology of Modern Societies*, Oxford: Blackwell, 1978.

Rocher, Guy, *Talcott Parsons et la sociologie américaine*, Paris: Presses Universitaires de France, 1972.

Róheim, Geza, *Origine et fonction de la culture*, trans. from the English by Roger Dadoun, Paris: Gallimard, 1972 (1st edn., 1943).

Rossi, Paolo, *Aspetti della Rivoluzione Scientifica*, Naples: Morano, 1971.

— *Immagini della Scienza*, Rome: Riuniti, 1977.

Rudner, Richard S., *Philosophy of Social Science*, Englewood Cliffs: Prentice-Hall, 1966.

Runciman, Walter Garrison, *Sociology in its Place*, Cambridge University Press, 1970.

Rusconi, Gian Enrico, *La Teoria Critica della Società*, Bologna: Il Mulino, 1968.

Ryan, Alan, *The Philosophy of the Social Sciences*, London: Macmillan, 1975 (1st edn., 1970).

Sahlins, Marshall, *Culture and Practical Reason*, University of Chicago Press, 1976.

— *Stone Age Economics*, London: Tavistock, 1974.

Sahlins, Marshall and Service, Ellman, *Evolution and Culture*, University of Michigan Press, 1960.

Sapir, Edward, *Selected Writings*, Berkeley: University of California Press, 1934.

Scheler, Max, *Die Wissensformen und die Gesellschaft*, Berne: Francke, 1960 (1st edn., Leipzig, 1926).

Schutz, Alfred, *The Phenomenology of the Social World*, trans. George Walsh and Frederick Lehnert, London: Heinemann, 1972 (1st edn., Vienna, 1932).

Scott, John Finley, *Internalization of Norms: A Sociological Theory of Moral Commitment*, Englewood Cliffs: Prentice-Hall, 1971.

Bibliography

Sebeok, Thomas, Hayes, Alfred and Bateson, Mary Catherine (eds), *Approaches to Semiotics*, The Hague and Paris: Mouton, 1972 (1st edn., 1964).

Sebeok, Thomas A. (ed.), *Current Trends in Linguistics, Vol. III: Theoretical Foundations*, The Hague and Paris: Mouton, 1966; *Vol. XII: Linguistics and Adjacent Arts and Sciences*, The Hague and Paris: Mouton, 1973, 3 vols.

Sebeok, Thomas A. (ed.), *Style in Language*, Cambridge, Mass.: MIT Press, 1960.

Seliger, Martin, *Ideology and Politics*, London: Allen & Unwin, 1976.

Simmel, George, *The Sociology of Georg Simmel*, trans. and ed. by Kurt Wolff, New York: Free Press, 1964 (1st edn., 1950).

— *Conflict in Modern Culture and Other Essays*, trans. Peter Etzkorn, New York: Teachers College Press, 1968.

— *On Individuality and Social Forms*, selected writings ed. by Donald Levine, University of Chicago Press, 1971.

Skorupski, John, *Symbol and Theory*, Cambridge University Press, 1979.

*Slater, Phil, *Origin and Significance of the Frankfurt School: A Marxist Perspective*, London: Routledge & Kegan Paul, 1977.

Smelser, Neil J., *Theory of Collective Behaviour*, London: Routledge & Kegan Paul, 1970 (1st edn., 1962).

Smith, Anthony D., *The Concept of Social Change: A Critique of the Functionalist Theory of Social Change*, London: Routledge & Kegan Paul, 1973.

Sorokin, Pitirim, *Sociocultural Causality, Space, Time*, Durham, North Carolina: Duke University Press, 1943.

Sperber, Dan, *Rethinking Symbolism*, Cambridge University Press, 1975 (French original, Paris, 1974).

Spinoza, Baruch, *Oeuvres complètes*, ed. by Roland Caillois, Madeleine Francès and Robert Misrahi, Paris: Gallimard (Bibliothéque de la Pléiade), 1967.

Stammer, Otto (ed.), *Max Weber and Sociology Today*, trans. by Kathleen Morris, Oxford: Blackwell, 1971.

Stark, Werner, *The Sociology of Knowledge: An Essay in Aid of a Deeper Understanding of the History of Ideas*, London: Routledge & Kegan Paul, 1967 (1st edn., 1958).

Steiner, George, *Extraterritorial: Papers on Literature and the Language Revolution*, Harmondsworth: Penguin, 1975 (1st edn., 1971).

— *After Babel: Aspects of Language and Translation*, Oxford University Press, 1975.

Steward, Julian H., *Theory of Culture Change: The Methodology of Multilinear Evolution*, Urbana: University of Illinois Press, 1973 (1st edn., 1955).

Stinchcombe, Arthur L., *Constructing Social Theories*, New York: Harcourt, Brace & World, 1968.

Sztompka, Piotr, *System and Function: Toward a Theory of Society*, New York: Academic Press, 1974.

Therborn, Göran, *Science, Class and Society: On the Formation of Sociology and Historical Materialism*, London: New Left Books, 1976.

— *What Does the Ruling Class When It Rules?: State Apparatuses and State Power Under Feudalism, Capitalism, and Socialism*, London: New Left Books, 1978.

Thompson, Kenneth and Tunstall, Jeremy (eds), *Sociological Perspectives*, Harmondsworth: Penguin, 1975 (1st printing, 1971).

*Todorov, Tzvetan, *Théories du symbole*, Paris: Seuil, 1977.

Toennies, Ferdinand, *Community and Association* (1887), trans. by Charles P. Loomis, London: Routledge & Kegan Paul, 1974 (1st edn., 1955).

Topitsch, E., *Vom Ursprung und Ende der Metaphysik: eine Studie zur Weltanschauungskritik*, Vienna: Springer, 1958.

— *Sozialphilosophie zwischen Ideologie und Wissenschaft*, Neuwied: Luchterhand, 1961.

Toulmin, Stephen, *The Philosophy of Science*, London: Hutchinson, 1967.

Touraine, Alain, *Production de la société*, Paris: Seuil, 1973.

Troeltsch, Ernst, *The Social Teachings of the Christian Churches*, trans. by O. Wyon of the German original, Tübingen, 1912, London: Allen & Unwin, 1931, 2 vols.

— *Der Historismus und seine Probleme*, Tübingen: Rolf Heise, 1922.

Turner, Victor, *The Forest of Symbols: Aspects of Ndembu Ritual*, Ithaca: Cornell University Press, 1967.

Tylor, E. B., *Primitive Culture: Researches into the Development of Mythology, Philosophy, Religion, Language, Art, and Custom*, London: Murray, 1871.

Unger, Roberto Mangabeira, *Knowledge and Politics*, New York: Free Press, 1975.

Verón, Eliseo, *Conducta, Estructura y Comunicación*, Buenos Aires: Nueva Visión, 1968.

Vico, Giambattista, *The New Science*, trans. Thomas Goddard Bergin and Max Harold Fisch, Ithaca: Cornell Paperbacks, 1970 (1st edn., 1948).

Vincent, Jean-Marie, *Fétichisme et société*, Paris: Anthropos, 1973.

— *La Théorie critique de l'école de Francfort*, Paris: Galilée, 1976.

Vincent, J.-M., Hirsch, M., Wirth, Alvater, and Yaffe, O., *L'Etat contemporain et le Marxisme*, Paris: Maspéro, 1975.

Volpe, Galvano della, *Logica come Scienza Positiva*, Rome: Ed. Riuniti, 1956.

Wallace, Walter L. (ed.), *Sociological Theory*, London: Heinemann, 1969.

Wallerstein, Immanuel, *The Modern World-System: Capitalist Agriculture and the Origins of the European World-Economy in the Sixteenth Century*, New York: Academic Press, 1974.

Weber, Max, *The Methodology of the Social Sciences*, trans. of part of *Gesammelte Aufsätze zur Wissenschaftslehre* (Tübingen: Mohr, 1922) by Edward A. Shils and Henry A. Finch, Chicago: Free Press, 1949.

— *Economy and Society: An Outline of Interpretive Sociology*, ed. by Guenther Roth and Claus Wittich of the work of several translators of *Wirtschaft und Gesellschaft* (Tübingen: Mohr, 1922; 4th enlarged edn by Johannes Winckelmann, Tübingen: Mohr, 1956), New York: Bedminster Press, 1968, 3 vols.

Bibliography

— *From Max Weber: Essays in Sociology*, trans. and ed. by H. H. Gerth and C. Wright Mills, London: Routledge & Kegan Paul, 1948 with many subsequent reprints.
— *Weber: Selections in Translation*, trans. by Eric Matthews and ed. by W. G. Runciman, Cambridge University Press, 1978.
Wellek, René, *Concepts of Criticism*, New Haven: Yale University Press, 1963.
*Wellmer, Albrecht, *The Critical Theory of Society*, New York: Herder & Herder, 1971.
Wells, G. A., *Herder and After*, The Hague: Mouton, 1959.
Westergaard, John and Resler, Henrietta, *Class in a Capitalist Society: A Study of Contemporary Britain*, Harmondsworth: Penguin, 1976 (1st edn., 1975).
White, Leslie, *The Science of Culture*, New York: Farrar, Straus, 1949.
— *The Evolution of Culture*, New York: McGraw-Hill, 1959.
Whitehead, Alfred North, *Science and the Modern World*, New York: Macmillan, 1967 (1st edn., 1925).
Wilden, Anthony, *System and Structure: Essays in Communication and Exchange*, London: Tavistock, 1972.
Wilson, Bryan R. (ed.), *Rationality*, Oxford: Blackwell, 1974.
Wissler, Clark, *Man and Culture*, New York: Crowell, 1923.
Wittgenstein, Ludwig, *Philosophical Investigations*, trans. by G. E. M. Anscombe, Oxford: Blackwell, 1968 (1st edn., 1953).
Wrong, Dennis H., *Skeptical Sociology*, London: Heinemann, 1977 (1st edn., New York, Columbia University Press, 1976).
Wrong, Dennis H. (ed.), *Max Weber*, Englewood Cliffs: Prentice-Hall, 1970.
Zeitlin, Irving M., *Ideology and the Development of Sociological Theory*, Englewood Cliffs: Prentice-Hall, 1968.
Zetterberg, Hans L., *On Theory and Verification in Sociology*, Totowa, New Jersey: Bedminster Press, 1963.
Zollschan, George K. and Hirsch, Walter (eds), *Social Change: Explorations, Diagnoses and Conjectures*, New York: Wiley, 1976 (1st edn., 1964).

Index

Index